Here's what they said about this book's outrageous predecessor,

SNEAKY FEATS:

"When it comes to big-time chutzpah, there's Evel Knievel, Gebel-Williams, and Superman. For the rest of us, there's *Sneaky Feats!*"
—*New York* Magazine

"Ebullient"
—*Saturday Review*

". . . astound and stupefy friends and family"
—Book-of-the-Month Club

"I wish I had thought of it first."
—*Village Voice*

and now,

MORE SNEAKY FEATS . . .

Books by Tom Ferrell and Lee Eisenberg

Sneaky Feats
More Sneaky Feats

Published by POCKET BOOKS

Are there paperbound books you want but cannot find in your retail stores?

You can get any title in print in POCKET BOOK editions. Simply send retail price, local sales tax, if any, plus 35¢ per book to cover mailing and handling costs, to:

MAIL SERVICE DEPARTMENT
POCKET BOOKS • A Division of Simon & Schuster, Inc.
1230 Avenue of the Americas • New York, New York 10020

Please send check or money order. We cannot be responsible for cash. *Catalogue sent free on request.*

Titles in this series are also available at discounts in quantity lots for industrial or sales-promotional use. For details write our Special Products Department: Department AR, POCKET BOOKS, 1230 Avenue of the Americas, New York, New York 10020.

TOM FERRELL and LEE EISENBERG

MORE SNEAKY FEATS

The Art of Showing Off and 49 New Ways to Do It

Drawings by
GIL EISNER

A KANGAROO BOOK
PUBLISHED BY POCKET BOOKS NEW YORK

MORE SNEAKY FEATS

Sheed & Ward edition published 1976

POCKET BOOK edition published August, 1977

This POCKET BOOK edition includes every word contained in the original, higher-priced edition. It is printed from brand-new plates made from completely reset, clear, easy-to-read type.
POCKET BOOK editions are published by
POCKET BOOKS,
a Simon & Schuster Division of
GULF & WESTERN CORPORATION
1230 Avenue of the Americas,
New York, N.Y. 10020.
Trademarks registered in the United States
and other countries.

ISBN: 0-671-81184-3.
Library of Congress Catalog Card Number: 76-10594.
This POCKET BOOK edition is published by arrangement with Sheed & Ward, Inc. Copyright, ©, 1976, by Tom Ferrell and Lee Eisenberg. All rights reserved. This book, or portions thereof, may not be reproduced by any means without permission of the original publisher: Sheed & Ward, Inc., 6700 Squibb Road, Mission, Kansas 66202.

Printed in the U.S.A.

To Sarah Ferrell
and Vanessa Jalet
for tolerating all this

Contents

PART TWO: CHEAP THRILLS WITH REAL MONEY

PART THREE: KNOT SO FAST, BUSTER!

PART FOUR: THE POWER TO CLOUD MEN'S MINDS

PART FIVE: LOOKY WHAT YOU MADE!

Not an Introduction

As the title of this book indicates, there was another one like it before. In the Introduction to that one *(Sneaky Feats: The Art of Showing Off and 53 Ways to Do It)* numerous historical parallels were adduced—from Cain and Abel through Daniel Boone, George Washington, Babe Ruth and Bobby Riggs—to demonstrate, illustrate, explicate and justify the role of the show-off in all stages of society hitherto discovered—especially now, and especially in America. The inference is clear: there is no real reason for another Introduction like that one.

Setting aside, therefore, the question of an Introduction, there remains the larger question of why there should even be a second and successor volume to the first. For one thing, this present book is published in recognition of the unanimously generous reception accorded to its predecessor. One reviewer, writing in the *Yale Daily News Magazine,* went so far as to say something like (we lost the actual clipping): "If you had the money to buy this book, you could probably buy something worse with it." No one has laid a glove on us yet—what more could we have asked?

Clearly, our message is getting through. To show off—to search for glory and recognition by learning to do things nobody else can do, and then finding ways to compel everybody else to watch you do them—is the vital element itself, the very stuff of which life is made. Look about you: all over the literate world, unprecedented feats of goldfish-swallowing and endurance-unicycle-riding are being conceived and executed for no other reason than to get their performers included in *The Guinness Book of World Records*. In every nation, literate or not, men and women strain every nerve and muscle preparing for the next Olympic Games, all of them hoping to run, swim, jump, or throw some kind of object faster, higher, or farther than ever before—and on television, if possible. Closer to home, hundreds of men and women in ridiculous costumes are lined up at this very moment in the effort to attract attention on "Let's Make A Deal." And as we write these words, the United States itself is engaged in a vast propaganda effort, sparing no technique of publicity or self-promotion, to make the world take heed that 1976 is its two-hundredth birthday. No one there is that doesn't love a show-off, or doesn't want to be one. It is in our blood.

Therefore this book. Once is never enough; if it were, there would be only one tower in the World Trade Center, instead of two; only one pyramid at Gizeh, instead of three; only one face carved out of Mount Rushmore, instead of four, or is it five?

The techniques of showing off that follow have been divided into significant sections, each calculated to teach you skills that will command, however unwillingly, the admiration and envy of spectators. The first of these, "Tricks for All Trades," provides an assortment of off-hand stunts, using simple props, that will make people fear and respect your name, whatever it is (and remember it, too). "Cheap Thrills with Real Money" shows you a number of ways, none costing more than a dollar, to raise rapid interest in your immediate vicinity. "Knot So Fast, Buster!" is a short course in manual dexterity with knots, strings, silk scarves, and whatnot, that will bind other people's attention inseparably to you. "The Power to Cloud Men's Minds" is a handy compendium of brain tricks, calculated to drive the audience of your choice stark bonkers. Finally, "Looky What You Made!" exhibits the show-off in his role as creator, making all manner of things to amaze and confound innocent bystanders, who probably wanted to be left alone, thank you.

Tom Ferrell
Lee Eisenberg

New York
January 1, 1976

PART ONE:

Tricks For All Trades

Tearing a Phone Book in Half

Here it is, fellow show-offs, the greatest strong-man stunt in history, all yours. And all you have to know in order to perform this trick is how to cheat. You're going to want to wait until summer before trying this one, because, as you'll see, you're going to want the windows open. You're also going to want to live in or near a big city where you can get some big-city phone books, because almost anybody can tear the Medicine Bow phone book in two without cheating.

To prepare, collect some dandy big phone books—the 1,700-page Manhattan is the classic. You're going to need some to practice on and some for performances.

Go into the kitchen, open all the windows, turn on all the fans, and set the oven at 350 degrees—no hotter, because you don't want the phone book to catch fire. Put the phone book in the oven and wait. How long you'll have to wait depends on how old and brittle your phone book is to begin with.

You must have all the windows open because baking phone books are smelly. It's not a repulsive rotten-egg killer smell, it's more like a fire in the basement. It will make you cough and your eyes will hurt, unless you keep the place well ventilated.

After about three hours, take the phone book out of the oven, using kitchen hot-pads so you don't get burned. This is a hot phone book now. Gingerly lift the cover and fold back the corner of a page to see if it's getting brittle. If it tends to crumble in your fingers, that's enough; if not, put it back in the oven until it is done.

When the phone book is done, put it in the back yard or out on the fire escape to cool. This will take a couple of hours all by itself, and by now the smell should have cleared out.

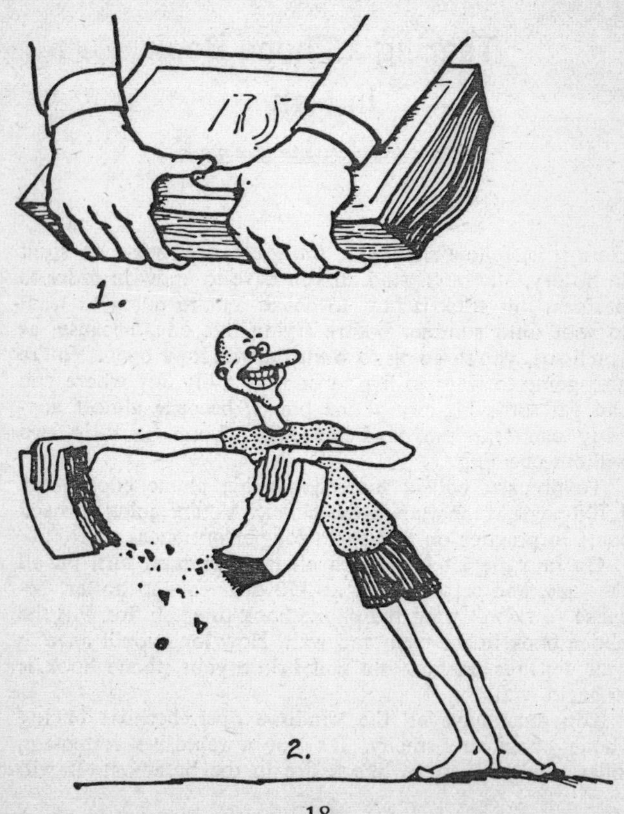

Ready? Pick up the phone book with the binding toward you. Hold the book as shown in figure 1, bending it slightly to bevel the pages so you start tearing one page at a time instead of the whole thing at once. Take a firm grip and give an enormous, slow, massive tug. Rrrrrrip! (figure 2).

If the phone book fails to go rrrrrrip, that's because you didn't cook it long enough. Remember that for your next effort.

When you have a supply of nicely baked phone books, just leave them around the house until some day when the neighbors are over. Then say, casually, "Betcha I can tear a New York (or Los Angeles, or Chicago) phone book in two."

Then, like the winner that you are, *Do it!*

A Belt Where It Hurts

You know how it drives you nuts when you're trying to learn something new—something new and not really worth doing, like long division or taking square roots—and you can't seem really to get the hang of it and it drives you wild with fury? Well, this is your opportunity to turn the tables on the world, with a stunt you can perform over and over on some hapless victim who should know better by now than to mess with an accomplished show-off. Fortunately for you, hapless victims never learn.

Here's what you do: you take off your belt (or bring an extra one along), double it in the middle, roll it up tight, and put it on a table. You invite an onlooker to stick a pencil (or a butcher knife, or a gilded dagger, or anything) into the center of the belt, so that when you try to snatch it away he will catch it by the loop in the middle. What could seem easier? Well, nothing is easier, as a matter of fact, since the first time he tries it he succeeds. Then you make your move: you bet him that he'll never succeed again. And as long as you follow these instructions carefully, he never will. You can snatch the belt away from the pencil again and again—he'll never find the middle in a million tries.

All right, here's how. Study carefully the drawing of the rolled-up belt. Remember, you double it in the middle first, then you roll it up in a tight coil toward the ends. Please note (this is important): the belt should be doubled before rolling so the tongue end will be on the outside of the coil, and a little shorter than the buckle end. Take off your belt and try it, you'll get the idea.

Now, every belt (anyhow, most every belt) has a shiny side and a suede side. If you fold and coil the belt as shown, the shiny side (marked A) will be the middle of the coil, and a pencil inserted at A will catch the belt when you try to snatch it, right? Right. Even a sucker should be able to figure this out, so let your victim succeed once. Next time, he'll put the pencil at A again. What do you do? Simple. Before jerking the belt, just let the tongue end unroll one turn. Then grab the two ends and pull. Letting the tongue end unroll one turn automatically changes the center of the belt from shiny side A to suede side B. Don't ask why. Just try it.

Of course, you may be working with a really dumb victim who can't even get it right the first time. In that case, now that you know the secret of switching the center

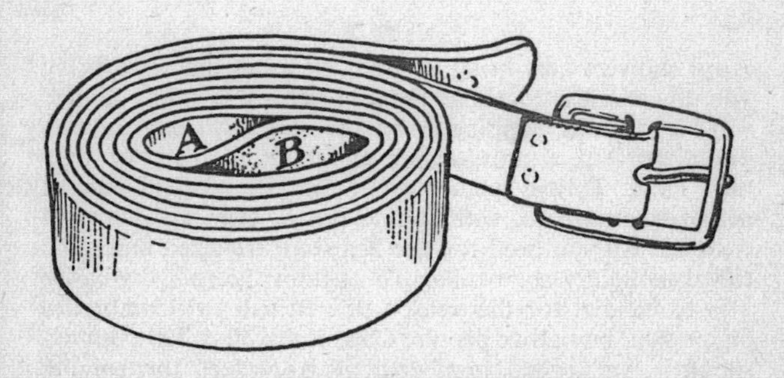

of the belt, you can rig it so he wins the first time. How many times you should let him win after that is up to your show-off conscience, and you probably know by now how hard-hearted that really is!

Strutting Behind the Bumbershoot

April showers may bring the rain, yes, but they also bring you the chance to shine. You've seen this many times: some cool dude bopping down the street twirling an umbrella, sort of a drum-major marching to his own one-man band. This is further proof that showing-off can be achieved anywhere, with simple props, even in inclement weather. All you need for this is a standard-sized umbrella, rolled as tightly as possible. The tighter the roll, the easier it is to handle; for this reason, the British twirl umbrellas better than any other people. Class is a well-rolled bumbershoot; a well-rolled bumbershoot is perfect for gaining respect. Here's how:

Hold the umbrella in whichever hand is most comfortable. You should grip it between your thumb and index finger (figure 1), about one-third down from the handle. The trick is to move the umbrella from finger to finger, cradling it in the crotches between the fingers.

Figure 2 shows the umbrella after it has been passed from thumb-index to index-middle. This exchange is made smoothly if you rotate your wrist gently as you pass the umbrella along. Try it a couple of times; five minutes is about all you need to get it down.

Figure 3 illustrates a slightly trickier exchange. You must get the umbrella over your index and ring fingers, held there by your middle finger. Again, keep rolling your wrist gently.

This final exchange is completed in figure 4. While expert twirlers can now twirl back the other way, the beginner may stop here, grabbing the umbrella with the palm of the hand. A nice final touch is to flip the umbrella into the air, then pluck it out of the air with the palm of the other hand. Anyone can do that, of course, so it's no big deal unless you've twirled the umbrella first.

Twirling an umbrella is much like twirling a baton. Girls should have an easier time learning than boys. But

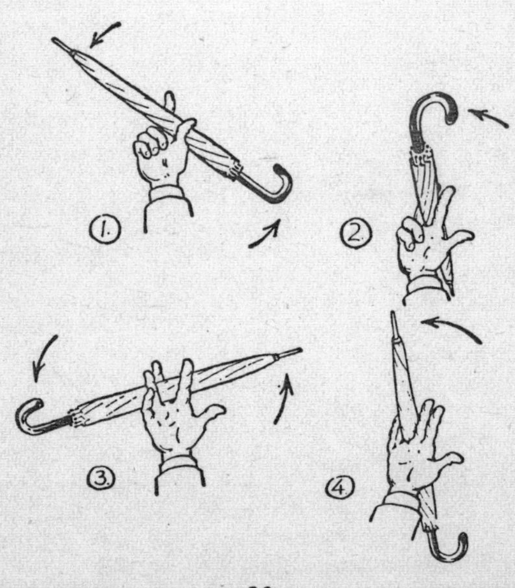

girls have to put away their toys when they grow up. Boys, on the other hand, can look forward to a lifetime of twirling in the rain. We don't say that's fair. All we do is teach showing-off, and let society determine the rest.

The Invisible Writer's Guide

Everybody wants to be a spy. Most spies these days are sponsored by governments, and have access to fancy equipment that only governments can afford. But the most fundamental weapon that every spy needs is within the reach of anyone. You too, no less than the C.I.A. or James Bond, can be a master of the art of secret writing. Secret writing is useful not only for communicating secrets to other show-offs who know how to read it, but also for writing down secrets that are too important to be left to memory; like the funniest jokes, the best secrets tend to be forgotten.

Of course, you could write down your secrets in some kind of fancy code, but then you'd have to remember the code. The best way, therefore, is to use invisible ink in the first place.

Fortunately, invisible ink is at hand, right there in the kitchen or at the grocery store. Grab yourself an orange or a lemon, cut it in two, and squeeze the juice out. There's your ink.

Now, using some handy tool, write your message on a

piece of paper. The cheapest instrument for this purpose is a toothpick, but a wet toothpick only stays wet long enough to write about one letter at a time. Better, if you can find one, is a pen like the one illustrated; the best place to find one is an artists' supply store. Get a pen that will not scratch the paper you're using, thus giving the enemy a clue to the location of your secret writing.

On no account borrow somebody else's fountain pen, because lemon juice will really gum it up something terrible.

As you write your message in lemon juice, you'll notice that you can, if you look carefully, see what you are writing. But in a few minutes, after the juice has dried, no visible trace remains. There! Your secret is safe.

When you want your secret back again, just heat the paper. The safest way to do this is with a hundred-watt or so light bulb. Just hold the paper very close to the hot bulb until the writing appears. The paper should not quite touch the bulb.

If you're in a big hurry to read your invisible writing, forget about the light bulb and heat the paper over a candle. Do *not* let it catch fire. When it's hot enough, the writing will appear out of nowhere, in brown ink.

If for some reason you can't find a lemon or an orange, milk will also work, but it's harder to write with and not

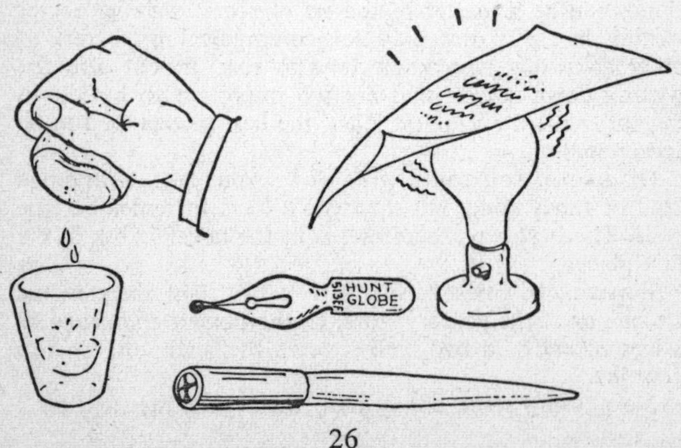

quite so invisible when dry. Besides, an international spy carrying a milk carton is easy for the bad guys to spot, whereas the lemon in James Bond's pocket hardly bulges at all.

Blowing Over a Wise Guy

There's a big difference between a wise guy and a show-off. A show-off, as we all know, is someone who exploits his natural or acquired superiority to gain power and glory and recognition. Can you spot the show-off in the picture? Right, it's the piglet. A wise guy, on the other hand, is somebody who uses big words that nobody understands. People who own big dictionaries and know how to use them are wise guys, like the wolf here. The next time you meet a wise guy, the way to vanquish him is to say: "Hey, wise guy, I bet you get all your long words from a dictionary. Listen, wise guy, I bet you can't stand your big dictionary on end and then blow it over. I bet you fifty cents and the loser has to write 'antidisestablishmentarianism' on the blackboard a million times."

The wise guy, of course, will say it can't be done; or else, since a wise guy hates to lose, he'll take a little sissy wise-guy puff at the dictionary. This will be followed by bigger huffs and puffs, until he blows his face red and falls over in total failure, which is about to happen to the wolf.

Then what? The brave, intelligent little pig—the show-

off, of course—whips from his inside pocket a large paper bag, which he folds neatly and places on the table, as shown in the smaller illustration. Then he stands the dictionary up on top of the paper bag. Finally, he blows up the paper bag with his breath, in the ordinary way. The dictionary, naturally, topples with a crash. The show-off is victorious.

Remember, if you want to be a show-off and not a wise guy, the mouth of the paper bag must be placed close to the edge of the table so you can get your own mouth into position to blow it up. If you have trouble at first, experiment with the placement of the big book on the bag until you've got it right; then, go forth and knock 'em flat! Or if you want to pursue the luxury route, instead of a paper bag you can use a long, fancy balloon from the five-and-ten. Either way, you'll be out in front of the wise guys and running.

Look, Ma, One Hand!

The show-off, always on the lookout for unique ways of impressing people, always asks whoever he meets to share any peculiar gimmicks, feats, or technical wizardry they might be hogging for their own personal glory. That's why we're able to bring you the wisdom of one Carmen Buccola of Garfield, New Jersey. Mr. Buccola, see, knows how to have a lot of fun with a bicycle wheel. It goes as follows:

Ask a chump if he can hold a bicycle wheel vertically with one hand—specifically, with one hand holding the wheel at the axle, as shown in the fantasy here. The chump will try it (which is why he's a chump in the first place) and find it very difficult indeed, no matter how strong he thinks he is. You then tell him you can hold the wheel at the axle, no matter how weak you really are. He laughs.

Then you have the last laugh.

The thing to do is grab the wheel with both hands, one on each end of the axle. Then—and this requires minimal practice—you give the wheel a strong spin with your fingertips.

When it's spinning vigorously, you can quite easily transfer the wheel to one finger and it will stay there, much as a toy gyroscope would. The wheel can even be balanced on the pinkie. Mr. Buccola even claims a six-year-old child can hold it.

Our thanks to Mr. Buccola for sharing his special knowledge; if everyone would get up off his bicycle seat and show off just once a day, this world would be a better place for all of us.

Standing an Egg On Its End

This wonderful stunt was contributed about five hundred years ago by Christopher Columbus, a notorious show-off who went on to discover America by sailing west until he fell off the end of the earth and landed here. One day Columbus and a bunch of the boys were whooping it up in a Seville saloon when Queen Isabella came in looking for her husband, a notorious rounder. Isabella had met Chris before because he was always asking her for money to fall off the earth with, so she went over to his table and asked if he could give her any information.

"Can I give you information!" Columbus cried. "I can even show you how to make a hard-boiled egg stand on end!"

"I bet you the *Niña*, the *Pinta* and the *Santa Maria* you can't," replied Isabella, forgetting all about her missing husband.

"Just watch," said Columbus smugly, and stood a hard-boiled egg on its end, right away, zip!

You can do the same stunt two ways. The modern way, which Columbus didn't know, is to pour a small heap of salt under the tablecloth, then replace the tablecloth and sort of scrunch the big end of the egg into that exact spot until a hollow develops in the mound of salt and the egg stands on end. If you do it this way you have to prepare the table in advance and not forget where the salt is. A brightly-patterned tablecloth helps to conceal the heap of salt.

But the old-fashioned Spanish way is simply to take the hard-boiled egg gently but firmly in your fist and bang its big end on the table until it's flat enough on the end to stand up. It's crude, but it worked for Columbus and it will work for you.

Queen Isabella was so impressed she coughed up the three ships without whining even once. Unless you can find a queen to astound with your eggmanship you'll probably have to settle for a smaller bet, but you'll win every bit as much admiration as Columbus did.

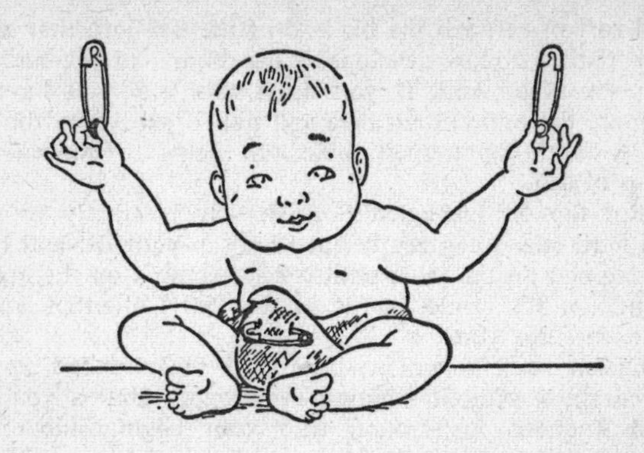

The Safety-Pin Swifty

See how fat and happy this baby looks? That's because he knows how to perform a fantastic show-off stunt that nobody on his block can figure out—especially not his mother, his father, or his two bigger brothers. You too can be fat and happy until you grow up if you just get two safety pins and follow these instructions very carefully.

What you do is this: you walk up to your mother, your father, your big brothers, or a perfect stranger, and exhibit two safety pins, interlocked and closed. You simply grasp one of the interlocked safety pins in each hand and pull them apart, zip, just like that. You hand over the safety pins for inspection and they are both still closed. Amazing? Yes. Apparently one pin passes right through the other. Since it is the nature of safety pins to stay closed—that's why they're called safety pins—it's very hard to see how you pull them apart. In fact it's impossible.

That is, it's impossible unless you study, very carefully, the diagram of the two safety pins. Take two safety pins, the bigger the better, and interlock them exactly, that's exactly, as the drawing shows. There are about a hundred ways to interlock two safety pins and ninety-nine of them are wrong. Only the way shown is right.

Now, grasp pin A at the bottom in your left hand. Grasp pin B at the bottom—that's the head of the pin, actually—in your right hand. Pull A and B in opposite directions, as shown.

You'll find, if you're careful, that this set-up allows pin A to unlock briefly as pin B passes through its mouth. Then pin A snaps shut again, without any effort on your part. Practice this slowly at first, so you see how it works; then swiftly, so nobody else can see what happens. If you get stuck, you're doing it wrong. Remember, safety pins are only safe compared to normal pins—don't forget they're sharp. Use this trick to stick your friends and family, not yourself!

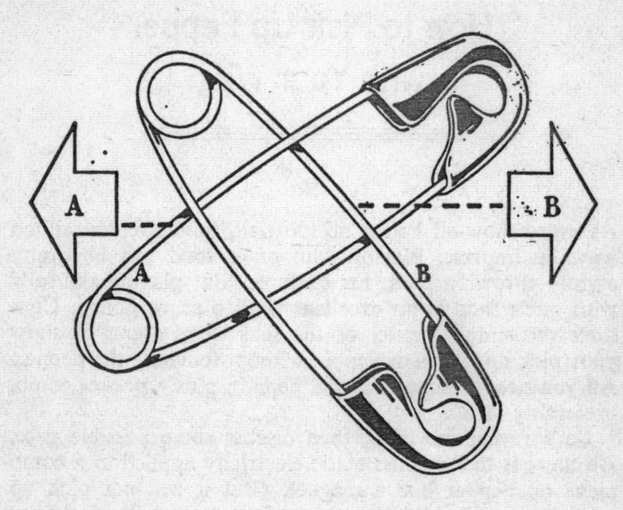

How to Pick Up Pepper with Your Wits

As every show-off knows all too well, food offers a million ways to impress. Playing with one's food can be pretty awful—throwing peas, for example. But playing skillfully with one's food is an excellent way to score points. Consider the simple beauty of the feat we're about to show you: pick up grains of pepper without touching the pepper. All you need is some salt and pepper, plus a pocket comb, preferably clean.

Let's reveal the trick, then discuss some possible uses. All there is to it is this: static electricity applied to a comb picks up pepper like a magnet. (But it will not pick up salt.) As every child knows, you generate static electricity by running a comb through your hair fast and furious. So put a comb in your pocket, call a friend, and propose you go out for a hamburger.

Once in the restaurant, take the salt shaker and sprinkle a pile of salt on the table or a plate. Then take the pepper shaker and sprinkle a generous portion of pepper over the salt. Your friend is sitting there watching, thinking you're a little nuts.

Now tell him you can remove all the pepper from the

mixture without touching it. If your friend says, "Now, why would you want to do that in the first place?" simply look philosophic and say, "Because it's there." This won't impress him much but it will at least hold his interest for a moment or so more.

Take your comb and run it through your hair. Place the comb over the mixture and, Zap! The pepper grains will leap up into the comb, while the salt crystals just sit there, as dumbfounded as your friend.

There are, of course, a million dumb variations. One is to pepper your food, then cry out, "Ouch! I've put on too much pepper!" Rather than use your fingers, you pull out your comb and despice your platter with the above-described technique. It may look pretty disgusting but showing-off sometimes involves the unsavory. We never promised you a spice garden, did we?

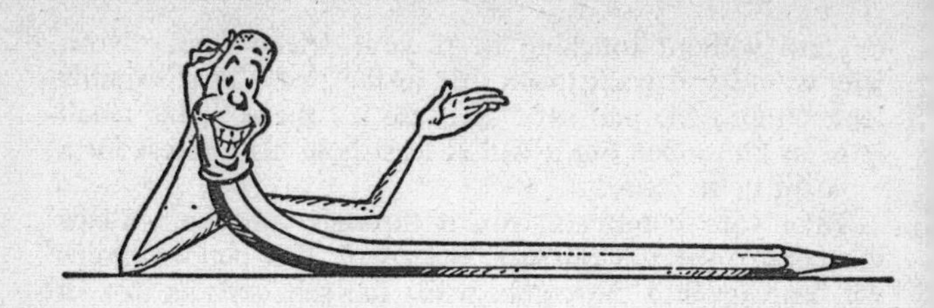

Thumb Fun with a Pencil

Nothing could be more open, more aboveboard, more obvious to the casual eye than this simple shifty little number. And, fortunately for the show-off, nothing could be harder to repeat from observation, or better adapted to driving your friends and enemies nuts by trying it themselves. It's one of those casual gestures that manage, somehow, to look like something they're not. You'll find it so easy to learn that you won't believe in its virtues until you let somebody else try it, and watch him or her turn all thumbs right in front of your laughing face.

To start, simply take a pencil—a full-length pencil, not a stub—and hold it under your thumbs with your palms together, as in figure 1 (note that the illustrations are drawn from your own point of view, not that of an observer).

Your next move is to cross your left thumb under your right thumb, as in figure 2, taking care to keep the forks of your two thumbs as close to each other as you can. This will result in the pencil starting to rotate clockwise, as the fingers of your right hand begin to glide over the fingers of your left hand. Your left hand begins to turn slightly palm down, your right hand a little more so.

The third position is shown (naturally) in figure 3. The thumbs are now parallel. The pencil has rotated about ninety degrees, and is held tightly pressed between the forks of the thumbs.

Now: continue the motion, using chiefly your left hand. The left thumb curls downward, then forward, around the pencil, and carries the pencil with it, until, at the end of the motion, the pencil is held in the thumbs below the hands, as figure 4 shows.

To reverse the motion, start by examining figure 5, which is shown as you would see it if you held your hands over a mirror. The thumbs are crossed—the right under the

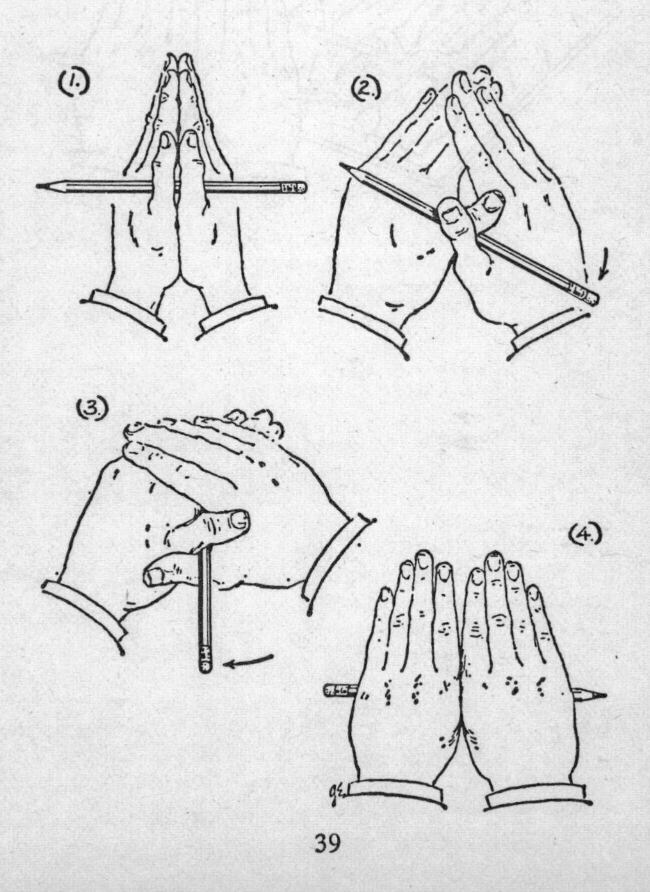

left—and the right thumb scoops the pencil off the left palm, resulting in a speedy return to figure 3. From here, just repeat the motion backward to figure 1.

Practice this until it all flows together in a single maddening motion. If you don't believe it's maddening, all right, don't believe! Just challenge a friend to do it with his own pencil, or better yet, a policeman with his nightstick. You'll find out, and so will they.

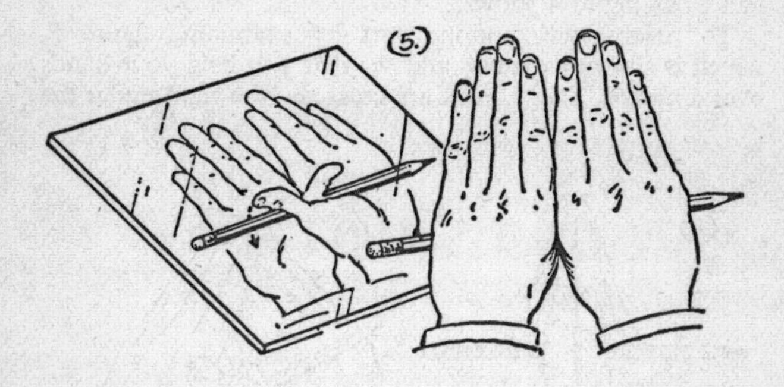

A Wall-to-Wall Card Stunt

Here's the picture. You get locked inside a room with your opposite number. You're a buyer and he's a seller. Or you're a spy for us and he's a spy for them. Or you're a lawyer for the defense and he's a lawyer for the prosecution. Or whatever. Your negotiations have broken down—and nothing—reason, anger, even begging—can convince this guy that he's wrong. There's nothing that can break the stalemate.

So you order lunch and, while you're waiting for its delivery, you pick up a deck of cards. You walk across the room and, nonchalantly, start sticking the cards up against the wall. The cards stay there. Your opposite number, fast becoming your chump, stares. You are showing off. He is breaking down. He tries a few himself, like the fellow here on the right. The cards slide down the wall and collect in an embarrassing little pile on the floor. What's going on here?

This fantasy goes to show how subtle showing-off can be. Start carrying a deck in your briefcase (or school bag, or tote bag, or lunch box). When the going gets rough, find yourself a room with a carpet of synthetic fibers. Without a lot of fuss, shuffle your feet on the carpet, then gently place a card on the wall. It will stick. Then give the deck to your chump. He'll try to match you. His feet won't shuffle. His card will slide. And so on and so forth, bearing in mind it all works better on a dry day.

We all know that this same technique will cause balloons to linger on a wall, but only a show-off would think of applying the principle to playing cards. No, this knowledge will not rescue the world from tragedy. It will, though, rescue you from boredom or failure. Is that anything to scoff at?

Baubles, Bangles and Dirty Tricks

For once, just for only once and never to be repeated, here's a show-off trick so low and rotten that it actually makes use of something up your sleeve. Most show-offs, most of the time, are too dignified and even honorable to make use of such a device; but there's a time for everything, sooner or later.

The time for this one is when you happen to own (or can buy reasonably cheap) two absolutely identical bracelets, or a reasonable facsimile thereof. Little glass bangles from the dime store will do fine. Of course, if you've got the class to own two identical expansion-band wrist watches, so much the better.

All right, put one of the bracelets (or wrist watches) up your sleeve—high enough to stick, but not so high you can't get at it in a hurry. Get a piece of rope two or three feet long. From here on out, just follow the pictures, like this:

Pick out some idle sucker who has nothing to do but let you deceive him. Walk up to him holding one bracelet and the rope and say, "Here, tie this rope between my wrists, and in the time it takes to say 'Harry Houdini,' I'll

DUPLICATE

put the bracelet on the rope, which is obviously impossible, right?"

Your sucker, being able to see the obvious, agrees. Quick as a flash, before he can say even the first syllable of "Harry Houdini," you turn your back on him, stick the bracelet in your hand deftly into some front pocket where it won't show, and slip the other bracelet off your wrist down into the middle of the rope.

If you're reasonably quick, you'll be finished long before your victim gets to the last syllable of "Houdini." But if you have trouble catching on at first, use "Bourke B. Hickenlooper" or "Department of Health, Education and Welfare" instead.

PART TWO:

Cheap Thrills With Real Money

The Pranky Hanky Coin Snatch

Making coins disappear is an indispensable star turn in the repertoire of every show-off. Of course, there are thousands of ways to make coins disappear, like swallowing them or dropping them down sewer gratings; but today's stunt is a lot niftier and less crude, and allows the performer to choose between just giving the coin back, or trying to outrun the original owner.

All right, here's how to pull it off. You need the following items: a small rubber band (the smaller the better); a big handkerchief (the bigger the better), or a scarf or dish towel; and a coin (borrowed from somebody who doesn't know any better).

Take the rubber band and wrap it around the fingertips of one hand, as shown in figure 1. The band should be snug, but not so tight that you can't easily wiggle it off your fingertips with a slight effort. Try it, and if it's too tight, get a looser band, or just wrap it around three or four fingers instead of five.

Holding the hand upright, drop the handkerchief over your hand so the rubber band is concealed. It will look like nothing more than an innocent handkerchief, right? Now, borrow the coin, tell your victim you're going to make it disappear, and stuff it, with your other hand, through the hanky into the middle of your rubber-band-wrapped fingertips, which form a sort of pocket to receive the coin (figure 2).

Everything should now be clear to you. You simply push the band off your fingers so it grabs the coin in the pocket. At the same time, you snatch the hanky into the air with your free hand, crying "Alakazam!" or some such. Of course, the coin and the rubber band cause a considerable lump in the handkerchief, so don't just stand there until somebody sees what's what; stick the hanky in your pocket right away.

It helps increase the mystery of this stunt if you already have a second, identical hanky in your pocket. Then, when your victim demands: "Hey, let me see that hanky," you can produce the innocent handkerchief and walk away with a smirk on your face and the coin in your pocket.

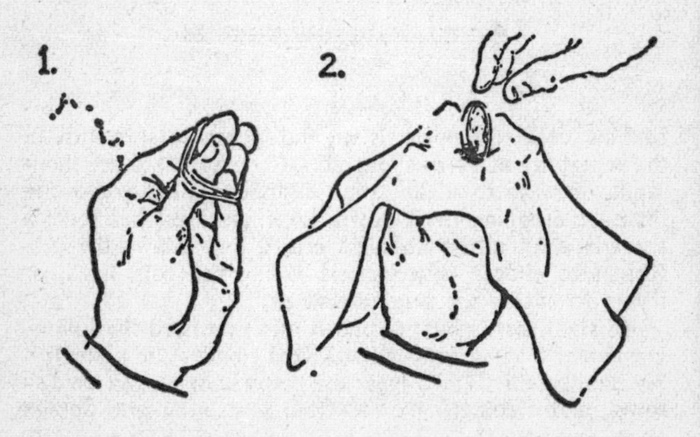

Put a Nickel in the Slot

Next to actually owning a great deal of money, the best way to show off with cash is to make flashy exhibitions of what money you've got. Disappearing-coin tricks are especially appropriate if you're a little short this week, since with a bit of fast patter you can borrow somebody else's coin and then make it disappear where only you can find it—later, of course.

To make coins disappear, it is first necessary to practice palming for a while. Professional magicians can palm coins like nobody's business, showing you first one side and then the other of the hand that holds the coin, without ever letting you see it. You don't have to be that good to be a show-off, but you should be able to learn to hold a coin somewhere in the palm of your half-opened hand without dropping it or looking at it. Everybody's palm is different—just experiment with the lumps and creases in your own palm until you find your own spot. Walk around for an hour with a coin in it until you feel comfortable.

Now, borrow a coin from somebody and say you're

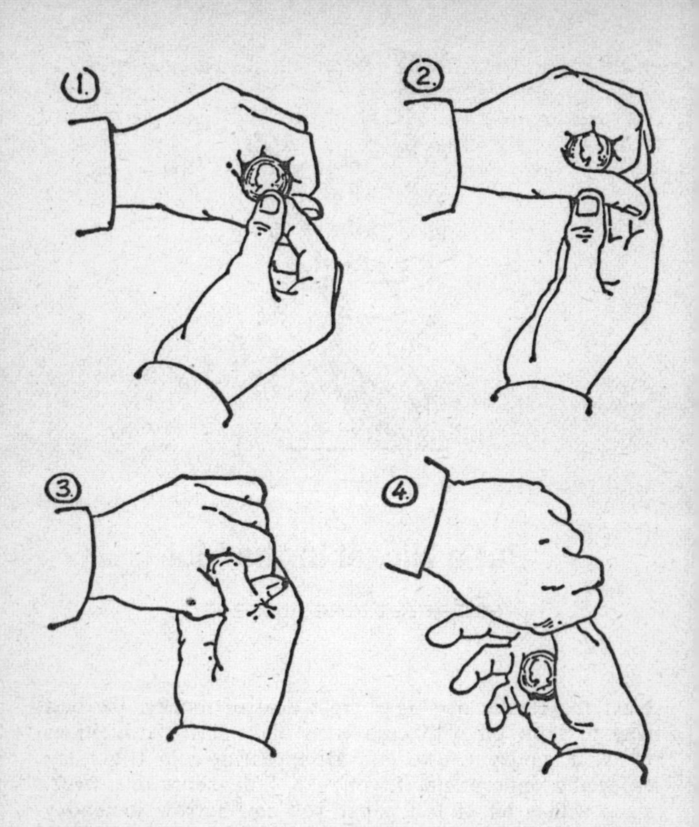

going to make it disappear. Hold out your left hand and make a fist, with the back of the hand upward. Leave a space in the middle of your fist about the size of the coin, and place the coin in it with your right hand (figure 1).

Position your right hand as in figure 2, and say you're going to push the coin into your fist until it disappears. When you're ready, push on the coin with your right thumb (figure 3). Note that your left fist is relaxed enough so that when the coin enters it, it's going to drop right on through into your right palm. The sucker who owns the coin, of course, is not going to notice this happening, especially if you're quick.

When the coin drops into your right palm, hold it there as you've learned to do (figure 4). Sweep your left hand into the air in an attention-grabbing manner and open it up with a cry of "Alakazam!" or "Zowie!" Remembering not to look at your right hand, stealthily get rid of the coin into your pocket.

Now, if you want to be a good guy and give the nickel back, that's your business—but if you don't, it's your nickel, if you're strong enough to keep it. That we can't teach you.

A Quarter's Worth of Deceit

The difference between a hard show-off trick and an easy one lies not in the skill required—anybody who can breathe in and out all day can handle the mechanical dexterity required for practically any reasonable stunt—but in the quality and quantity of the deception required to go along with the manipulation. Fortunately, ninety percent of showmanship lies simply in believing you're going to get away with what you're about to try; and if you didn't have that simple faith in your own superiority, that little voice inside your head that tells you you're a winner, you'd never be a show-off in the first place. Therefore, this lesson is slightly harder than most, but we've added a free extra simple trick at the end for those times when nothing seems to work for you. Start in on the hard part by plopping a quarter in the palm of your right hand and just looking at it for a moment, as in figure 1.

Reach for the coin with your left hand while turning the back of your right hand toward the audience—nothing obtrusive now, just a slight twist, enough to obscure their view of the coin a little (figure 2). Now, appear to grab the

coin with your left hand. Here's where belief in yourself comes in, because you've got to make a tight fist around the imaginary coin, while making a loose and flabby fist with your right hand where the real coin remains.

Keep your eyes, and everybody else's attention, on the left hand, and everybody but you will believe—such is the power of suggestion—that the coin is in your left hand where you're pretending it is. You can help out the illusion by pointing at your left hand with your right, being careful, of course, not to actually let go with your right (figure 4).

Snap your left hand open. No coin! (figure 5). Everybody will think you've made it disappear and everybody will fall down with admiration, provided you practice the whole sequence of moves in front of a mirror until they blend smoothly together, and also provided you really and truly act as if you too believed you had transferred the coin to the left hand. As soon as you can fool yourself, you're ready to go forth and perform.

Okay, that's the hard part. Now that you have it down pat, relax a little by pushing your quarter through a nickel-sized hole. Impossible, you say? We wish it were, because we still can't figure out how it works, and neither will anybody else you may be trying to impress with your command of spare change.

Anyhow, all you need to do is crease a piece of paper, then trace a nickel in the middle of the crease and cut out the hole (figure 1).

Try putting a quarter through the hole. Nothing doing, right? Very well, crease the paper as in figure 2 and drop the quarter into the hole, where it falls about halfway through. Then simply flex both ends of the paper upward a little (figure 3), the hole mysteriously elongates, and the quarter falls right through, plop. And plop will go anybody who told you it couldn't be done, especially if it was their quarter and you had a bet on it.

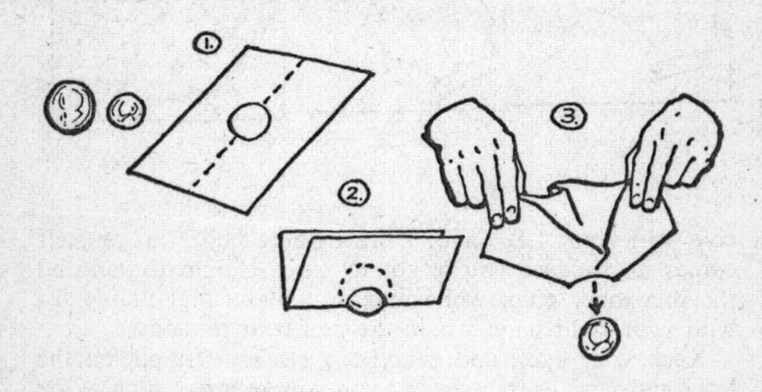

A Money-Mad Manipulation

If you have wowed an assembled audience by rolling a quarter back and forth across your knuckles, and some wise guy asks you what you do for an encore, you, the show-off, better have one. Well, this is it. You will require nothing more than a few coins and your own fingers. The manipulation is a bit more difficult than rolling a coin across your knuckles, though it doesn't look like it. On this you're really going to have to practice. If you have trouble, don't blame it on us. We have tried it and it works. So there!

The problem is to hold four coins with your fingers and, using one hand only, reverse the order, putting the first coin at the end, then repeating the process again and again.

Figure 1 shows the correct starting position. You hold the coins with your thumb, index, and middle fingers. Hold them easily, without too much pressure.

The second step requires you to let the coin in front slide down a bit, your ring finger now coming into play

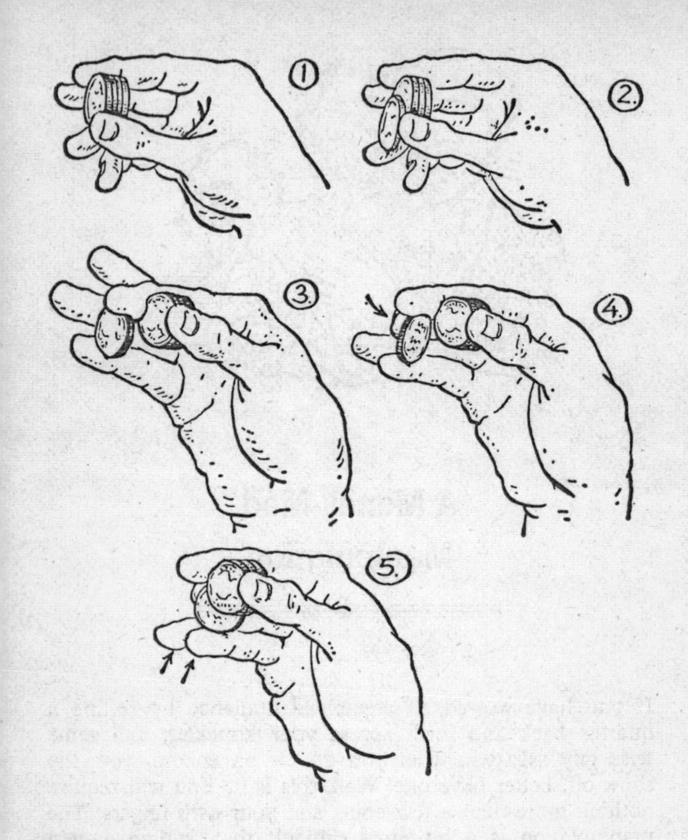

and keeping the coin from dropping altogether. This is shown in figure 2.

Figure 3 shows further progress. The coin you're moving is grasped between your middle finger and pinkie, with the ring finger being cooperative and helping out as much as it can. What you want to do now is start revolving the coin back toward the end of the stack.

Figure 4 shows the proper direction. Begin to guide the coin toward your palm as the arrow indicates.

To avoid dropping the coin at this critical juncture, keep the coin propped with your pinkie directly beneath it. Keeping your hand and nerves as steady as possible (watch it!), bring the coin back behind the stack and put it in place. Now you are ready to repeat the operation with the next coin.

Practice hard, maintain clean living, and have faith: if you do these three things—especially the first—you will soon be moving coins around with the agility of a Nureyev.

The Invaluable One-Dollar Ring

Ken Geisel, a show-off from Clifton, New Jersey, goes around gaining respect and admiration just because he has this magic ring, see. Well, it's not really a magic ring, but it *is* made out of solid money and it's certainly worth its weight in cold cash. All you need to make it is a dollar and the manual dexterity of a six-year-old. If you're seven and have a fifty-dollar bill, that's okay too—even better, in fact. No matter—knowing how to make a nifty ring out of a bill is a fine way to impress kids, also a surefire way never to be caught someplace with just lint in your pocket. Any cashier will gladly take this ring on your finger and give you a decent return in hock.

Take a nice fresh bill and place it in front of you (figure 1). Fold up the bottom edge, forming a lip with the bill's white edge, as in figure 2. Now fold the bill in half from the top down, tucking it under the white lip. Easy? Figure 3 points the way.

Figure 4 has you folding the bill once again, but this time don't tuck it into the lip. Just leave it cleanly folded.

Now you are about to turn all this folding into a ring of proper size. Take the left side of the folded bill and form a ninety-degree angle (figure 5). Following the dotted arrow in figure 5, bring the right side around the vertical section, and stop when you're approximately ¾ of an inch past it (figure 6). Make sure you are adjusting properly for the size of your finger.

Now, following the arrow of figure 6, fold down the vertical part and fold it up behind the face of the ring.

Take the ¾ inch or so piece and bring it around in

front of the face, tucking it in where shown (figure 7). This will keep the ring together. A little practice, and you will have the neat little item shown in figure 8. A dab of Scotch tape behind may be cheating, but it can help a lot.

The Great Coin Chase

It's more important than ever these days to be able to keep track of your money. This stunt enables you to keep track of your small change with a feat of astonishing mentalism that may make your enemies so mad they'll throw anything that's loose—including their pocket money. You could clean up.

Here's what happens: you place three coins in a row and turn your back. You challenge a bystander to turn one coin over, then switch the coins around as many times as he likes, then turn the selected coin back the way it was. You take one look at the coins and tell him which he turned over. It never fails—provided you follow these instructions, and you can get your victim to follow yours. Here's how:

Take three coins of different values—say, a nickel, a quarter, and a dime. Write on a sheet of paper the numbers 1, 2, and 3 in a neat row, then lay out the coins below the numbers as in the illustration—all heads up. Put the dime on 3, as shown. Now you're ready to turn your back. Remember, the dime is on 3. This is important! Got it? The Magic Number is 3!

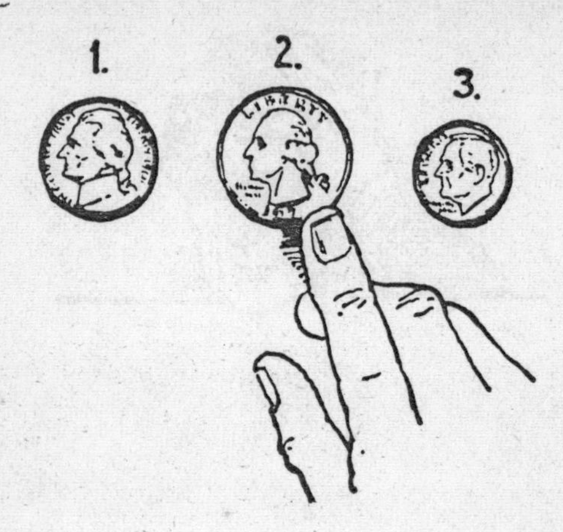

Tell your sucker to turn any one coin to tails. When he's done that, tell him to switch the other two—the ones he did *not* turn over—with each other.

When he's done that, tell him to switch any coins with each other as many times as he likes—but he must tell you which ones he switched—1 and 3, 2 and 1, whatever, while you listen carefully.

Here's what you're listening for. You're trying to follow the transformations of your Magic Number—which was 3 to start with. However, if 1 and 3 are switched, the Magic Number becomes 1. Then if 1 and 2 are switched, it becomes 2; if 2 and 3 are switched, it's now 3 again; and so on. Got the idea? Just follow the number. It helps to use your fingers.

When your subject says he's switched enough coins, tell him to take the one he turned to tails and turn it back to heads. Now with your Magic Number, whatever it is, firmly in mind, turn around and look.

The first possibility is that the Magic Number has the dime on it. If this is the case, the dime is the coin that was turned over.

The second possibility is that the Magic Number does not have the dime on it. If this is the case, then the coin on the Magic Number, whatever it may be, is *not* the coin that was turned over. The dime, whatever it may be, is also *not* the coin that was turned over. There is only one coin left, and *that* is the one.

Alive with pleasure!

Newport

©Lorillard, U.S.A., 1976

18 mg. "tar", 1.2 mg. nicotine
av. per cigarette, FTC Report Dec. 1976.

Warning: The Surgeon General Has Determined That Cigarette Smoking Is Dangerous to Your Health.

Warning: The Surgeon General Has Determined That Cigarette Smoking Is Dangerous to Your Health.

11 10 9 8 7 6

True lowers tar to only

5 MGS. TAR

And has a taste worth changing to.

Regular: 5 mgs. "tar", 0.4 mgs. nicotine, av. per cigarette, FTC Report Dec. 1976.

©Lorillard, U.S.A., 1976

There is no third possibility. It would seem that there should be, but there isn't, which is one reason this whole trick is so maddening. Can you figure out how it works? We can't, but show-offs don't know absolutely everything—just how to drive people nuts, and with this trick and three coins you're in the driver's seat.

A Linkup in Space

While Russian and American astronauts were joining each other in outer space a while ago, show-offs could only stand around with their hands in their pockets while governments got all the headlines. Here, now, for show-offs too poor to afford Apollo capsules, is a space-linking trick that will make you famous throughout the block you live on, and will only cost between one dollar and nothing at all. Besides, the dollar, if you have one, can be recycled for any use of your choice later on.

Your required astronaut equipment consists of a dollar bill and two paper clips. A strong piece of paper of the same size and shape can be substituted for the dollar.

Start by folding one-third, more or less, of the dollar behind the rest, as shown in figure 1. Then take one of the paper clips and put it over the fold, as in figure 2.

Still following figure 2, fold the left end of the dollar over to the right. Put the other paper clip over the new fold, as shown in figure 3. Note that the second paper clip is placed to the right of the first; also note that the second clip is placed only on the top and middle layers of the

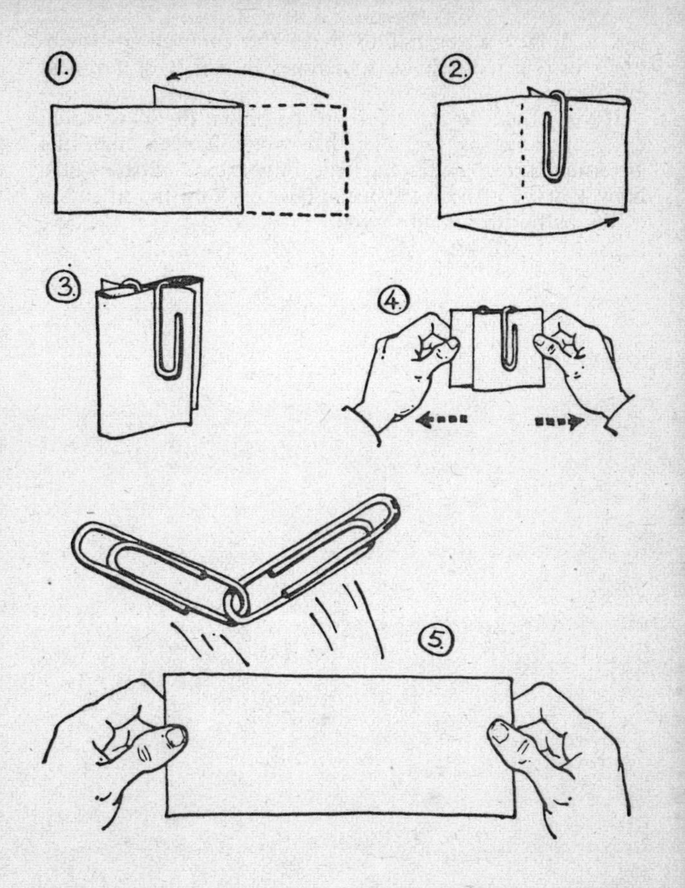

folded dollar. It does not, repeat *not,* fit over the bottom layer as well.

Now, grasp the two ends of the dollar and start counting down (figure 4). When you reach zero, pull the dollar out flat, as in figure 5. With a sharp click, the paper clips will spring into space, much harder than you probably think as you're reading this. What's more, they will be linked together, as the illustration shows. How come? That's classified information.

You can try this with additional folds and more paper clips on the dollar. About four is as many as there is room for, and they never fail to make the connection—sometimes in one long chain, sometimes in a sort of formless jumble.

If you could do this trick on the moon, the clips would fly four times as far, but that won't happen until the government recognizes the true importance of show-offs. Now that you know the techniques, getting the attention of the authorities is up to you.

The Five-Cent Solution

Otho C. Woods must be the biggest show-off in Whittier, California. Not long ago he sent us a nice letter in which he set down no fewer than eight sneaky feats, all of them worthy of your attention. Unfortunately, we only have room to pass one of them along. Total cost for props is five cents, for all you need is a nickel. And this is what you can do with the nickel. You can tell every time, even with your back turned, whether a nickel spun on a hard surface comes up heads or tails, just like the fellow in the drawing here is doing.

Mr. Woods's technique is so simple we're ashamed we didn't think of it ourselves. For this nickel business depends on a little nick, a nick you apply to the nickel with any hard material—a sharp stone, for example, or a file. Take the stone and etch a nick into the edge of the coin, either on the heads side (as shown in the inset) or tails, whichever you prefer. Now, in some very private place, where there is a hard-surfaced table, preferably one with a glass top, spin the nickel on its edge and, as the nickel slows down and begins to stop, listen very carefully. If the nickel falls on the side on which you've put your nick, it will give off a distinctly different sound than on the other, nickless side. You have to practice to hear the difference;

it's a fairly subtle difference and practice is necessary for you to distinguish it. We can't really tell you what it sounds like, but, well . . . keep spinning that nickel and you'll hear what we mean.

Once you are able to hear the difference between heads and tails, go out and find your audience. Tell them you have psychic power to determine heads and tails. Take the nickel from your pocket, turn your back, and tell them to spin the coin on the table.

With unerring accuracy, you will reveal heads or tails, much to the amazement of your fans. You might bet them a milkshake you can call the side twenty times in a row. And you can call it till the cows come home if you have that much free time.

The Inside-Outside Coin-and-Hanky Pass

Here's a little number you can turn to when you're down to your last nickel and clean handkerchief; those with half a dollar and a posh restaurant napkin are not, however, forbidden to play. The only thing that might put you off is your sense of the fitness of things, what non-show-offs call the Moral Sense. Since the illusion is achieved by such a fundamentally dumb trick, you may be ashamed to use it; but since it always works, you probably won't.

What appears to happen is simple enough: you push a coin right through a handkerchief, without making a hole or even much of a fuss.

What really happens is even simpler. Just follow the pictures. Start by picking up a coin between thumb and forefinger of the left hand (figure 1). Now, drape a hanky over the whole works *but,* as you do so, be sure to push a little dimple into the top of the hanky, so a small fold is caught between your thumb and the coin (figure 2).

Now comes the silly part. Flip back the front half of the hanky, to prove the coin is still underneath (as the arrow in figure 3 shows). Then, with a flick of the wrist,

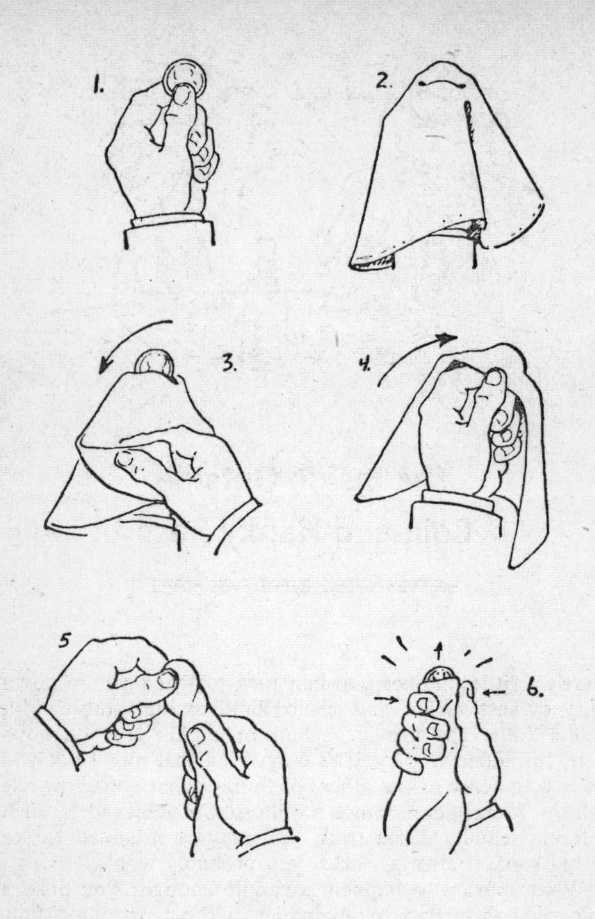

snap not only the front half of the hanky but also the back half forward over the coin (figure 4).

This looks as though, having exposed the coin, you're just covering it up again; but in fact, it results in more or less turning the hanky inside out, so to speak, so the coin is now held between your index finger and thumb, barely concealed behind the bottom fold of the hanky. The bulge at the top of figure 4 is the coin.

Now, twist up the hanky to show the spectator how tightly the coin is wrapped up in it (figure 5). When he's convinced, just squeeze the edges of the coin through the hanky, and it will squirt right out (figure 6).

Shake out the hanky to prove it is undamaged, and put the coin in your pocket. After a workout like this, you probably deserve it.

PART THREE:

Knot So Fast, Buster!

Tying a Knot with One Hand

Why should you learn how to tie a knot in a silk scarf with one hand, in a single deft manipulation? How can you ask? Everything you know how to do that nobody else can do is part of your show-off routine. How many of your friends, leaning against the candy store in midafternoon, can come up with anything as nifty as this? Be the first one on your block. And if you don't have a silk scarf, you can use a necktie or even, if worst comes to worst, a piece of string.

Here's how: Using both hands, roll the scarf loosely and lay it across one hand (we are using the right one for demonstration purposes), as shown in figure 1. If there's any difference in the length of the ends, the longer one should be toward you, on the front of your palm.

Now, clip the dangling end of the scarf, the one that's in front of your palm, between your fourth and pinkie fingers (figure 2). Notice the end of the scarf marked A in the drawing. That's not the end you've grabbed with your pinkie, it's the other end. Pay attention carefully to end A so you don't get lost in the next step. Ready?

Roll your hand toward you so the palm goes down and

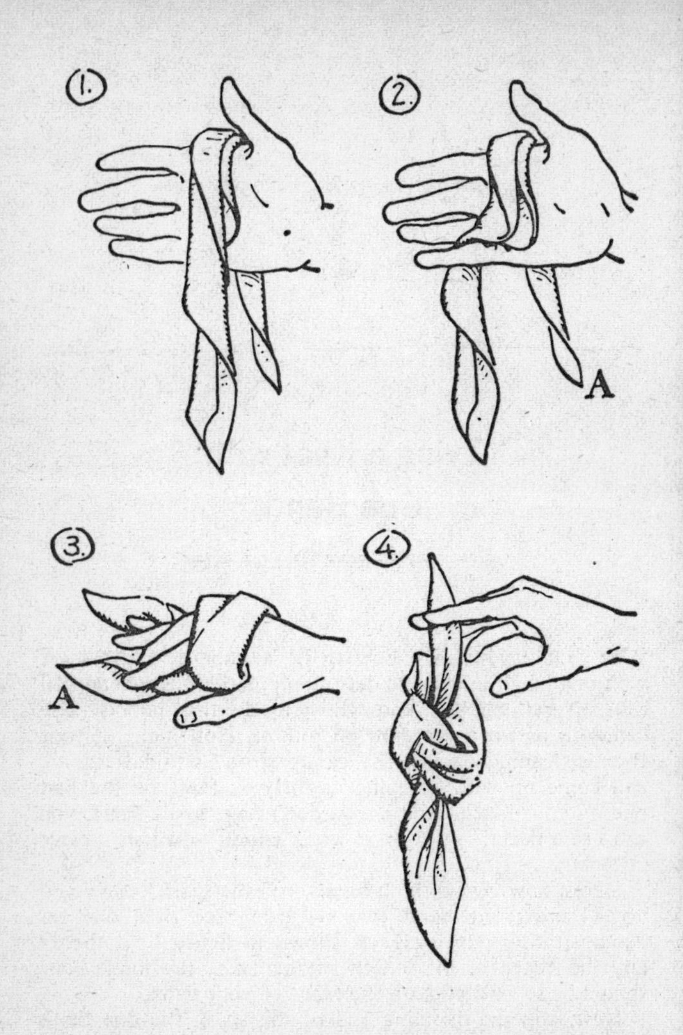

the back goes up, until, with your index and middle fingers, you can reach around and grab the end marked A. When you've got it, you'll find that the scarf is loosely wrapped once around your hand, with one end of the scarf held between index and middle fingers, and the other between the fourth finger and the pinkie. The scarf should be a loose fit on the hand, not a tight one. You are now ready to astonish yourself and others with the final step.

Let go with the fourth and pinkie fingers. At the same time, keeping a firm hold at A with index and middle fingers, give your arm and wrist a snap downwards so the scarf falls forward off the hand. You now have figure 4, the scarf with a knot in it.

After a little practice, you'll be able to perform the whole number in a single swift motion. Then you can set out to amaze the neighbors, the candy store, finally the whole block. Tomorrow, the world!

Slipping the Cuffs

The greatest professional show-off of all time, Harry Houdini, made his living by being chained up in handcuffs and ropes and so on and locked in trunks and dropped to the bottom of rivers. After a few minutes he would rise to the surface not only free and alive but dry all over. The average show-off can't do such heavy tricks and hadn't better try, but here's a dandy escape number to provide endless hours of entertainment for the show-off's friends and frustration for his enemies. We learned it from Bruno Profumo, an Englishman who passed through our country giving lessons in one-upmanship not long ago.

Take two people—a boy and a girl are best, for obvious reasons. Tie a piece of string two or three feet long between the wrists of one person; then tie a similar piece of string between the wrists of the other, being careful first to cross the strings once only, so the two people are linked together as in figure 1. Be careful not to tie the strings too tight, but tight enough so the hands can't slip out.

Now, challenge the two people to get out of this mess without untying the knots or cutting the string. Let them

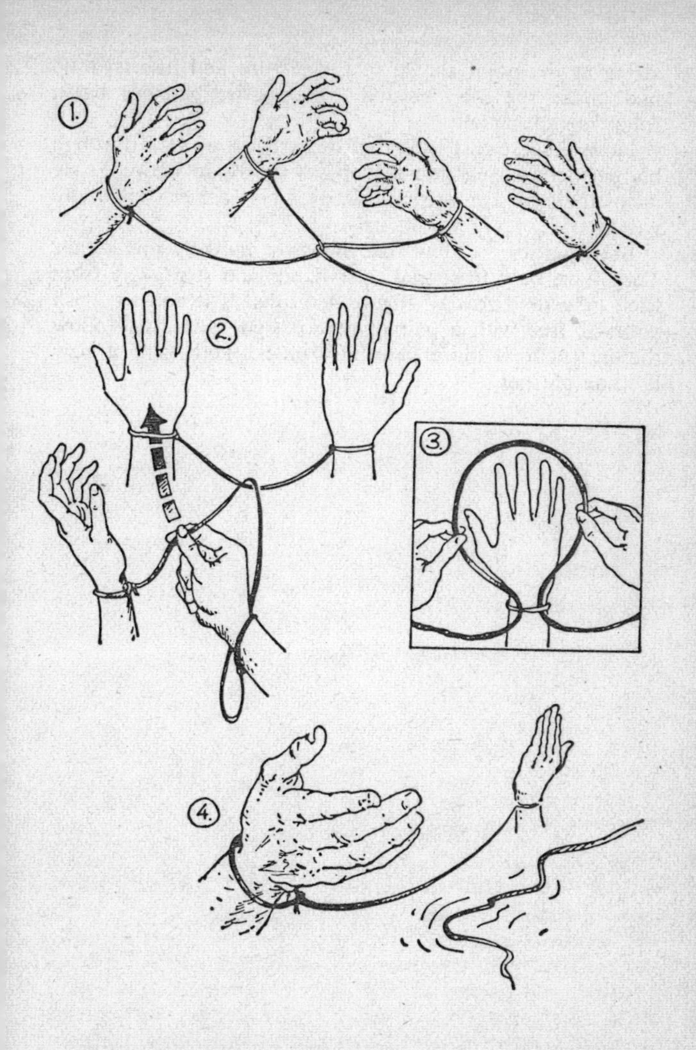

try. The more they try, the more fun it becomes. You'll get the idea after a few minutes of experimentation.

When they've had enough, refer to figure 2, which is drawn from the point of view of one of the two intertwined victims of this trick. Let one person just put his hands in the air and do nothing; the other grasps his own string at the point shown in the picture and inserts it up and under the loop around the opposite person's wrist, following the arrow.

Now the escapist pulls his own string upward through his partner's string into a loop, as shown in figure 3. He drops the loop away from him, over his partner's hand and wrist.

Both parties are now free, however unlikely this seems. They have only to spread their hands and step away from each other and zowie!—figure 4 results. If it doesn't, slash yourself free with a pair of scissors, go back, and follow the instructions more carefully, unless you want a new lifetime partner.

Spooling Around

Here's a work of great wonder that can be performed by any show-off with access to a sewing box. If you don't own a sewing box, you probably know someone who does; your mother will love you all the more when she sees what splendid things can be done with material ordinarily useful only for replacing buttons!

What seems to happen is: you present some spools, the ordinary sewing-thread kind, which have been threaded on two strings, as in figure 1. Any number of spools will do, from one on up, but we're showing three spools, a nice number to start with. You place a big handkerchief, a towel, or a scarf over the spools, and mess around briefly underneath it (figure 2). Then, with a grand flourish, you jerk the strings and plop! The spools all fall off, but, amazingly, the strings are unbroken. Fantastic!

What really happens is shown in figure 3. Look carefully at the middle spool. As you see, the two pieces of string are not what they seem to be in figure 1. The trick is prepared by taking two pieces of string and tying them together in the middle with one tiny loop of white thread—there it is, right in the center of figure 3. The

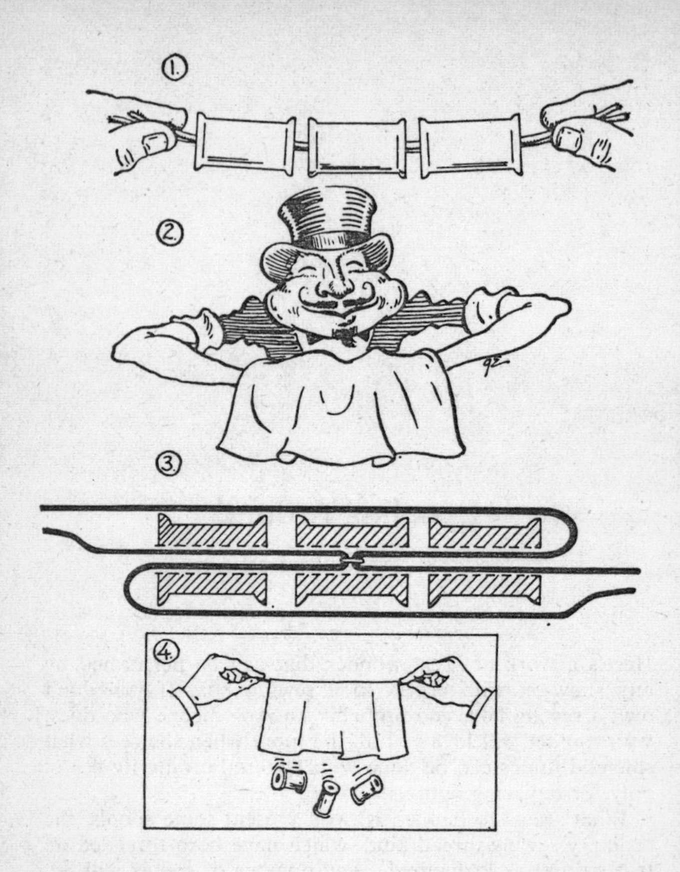

spools are then threaded on the strings so the whole affair looks like figure 1.

Now, drop the hanky over the spools—if you don't have three hands, you may want an assistant here—and simply switch the ends of the strings under cover of the handkerchief. The correct arrangement of the ends of the strings is shown in figure 3. The strings should be long enough so that they stick out from underneath the hanky when you're finished.

All right, now jerk the strings (figure 4). The tiny loop of thread breaks, the strings simply whiz out of the spools, and the spools fall free. You can even let an onlooker jerk the strings for you, as long as you don't let him peek beneath the hanky.

Hand over the strings to a spectator for inspection; the broken thread is so tiny it will escape notice as it falls to the floor. Give the spools back to your mother and bask in her attention as she tries to figure out where she got a kid as smart as yourself!

Tying One On

Every show-off despises anyone who gets caught doing things the easy way when he could be seen doing them the hard way. The bow tie is the case in point. Anyone can wear a bow tie of some sort: there are clip-ons, snap-ons, probably even a glue-on somewhere. While these are certainly convenient, they are definitely not worthy of your respect, because the man who knows not how to tie a bow tie is a man without sunshine—or without something, we're not really sure what. In any event, hand-tied bow ties look more impressive than ready-mades, your selection is greater, and since it's easy to do in the first place, why not learn? Tying a bow tie is like tying your shoes—exactly. Follow these easy steps. Bear in mind the drawings represent your image in a mirror. That way it'll be easier to follow.

One end of the bow tie should start off longer than the other, as shown in figure 1. Take the left end and drape it an inch or so longer than the right.

Figure 2 has you bringing the left under and over; figure 3 shows you tightening the tie around your neck.

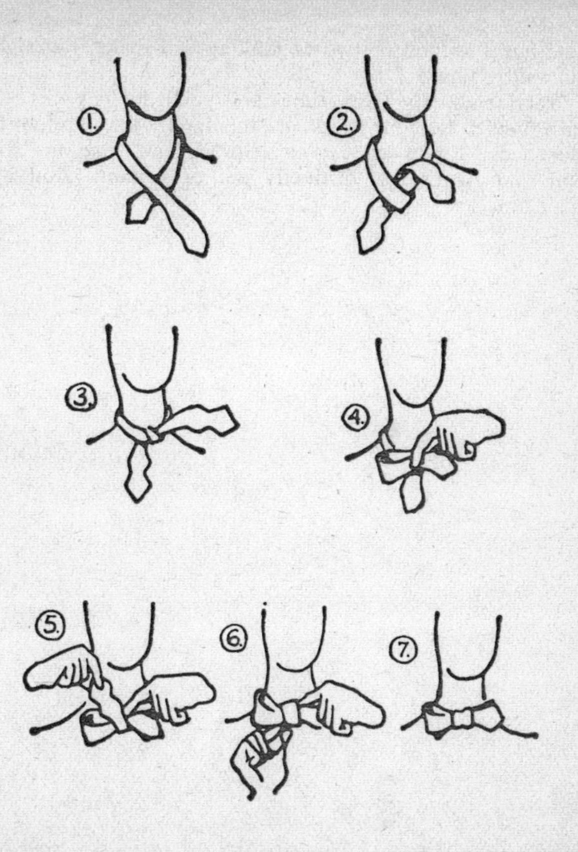

Using your right hand, fold the end you've brought under and over into what looks like the beginning of a bow tie, figure 4. Hold it there with your index finger.

Now with your left hand, take the end hanging straight down and bring it up and over the fledgling construction, figure 5. Keep a loop open with your right thumb.

The next step is a hard one, so listen. Your mission is to push the end you've just brought over through the loop being held by your right thumb. Just shove it through there and pull halfway through and as tight as you can, figure 6. At this point the knot is technically complete, but ugly and messy. Do not give up!

All that remains is the fixing up. Your bow tie is complete but a second or two of fiddling will make it straight and spiffy, figure 7.

Practice all this a few times and you'll hit pay dirt. Or learn how to tie your shoes and then apply that wisdom to your neck. Either way, your clip-ons and snap-ons will soon find themselves distinctly out of fashion. And it's about time.

Kiss a String and Make It Well

In addition to nimble wits and lightning fingers, the show-off's most useful tool, when all's said and done, is his mouth. Today's stunt will show you how to perform a miraculous feat with, apparently, no other tool but your mouth—the bigger the better.

What appears to happen is that you approach a sucker, holding a doubled loop of string. You hold it out to him and ask him to cut it (of course you hope he's got a pair of scissors right there in his pocket). When he cuts through the doubled loop, you release one of the cut loops and stick the other in your mouth; then, presto, you pull the cut ends out of your mouth and they have, altogether miraculously, joined together.

Here's how it happens. Remember, we're showing it to you from your own point of view as you work it. Remember, also, we're showing you a great deal more of the trick than your sucker is supposed to see. This applies especially to figure 4, as you'll note when we get there.

Take a nice clean piece of string, maybe two feet long, and tie it into a loop. Give the loop half a twist forward

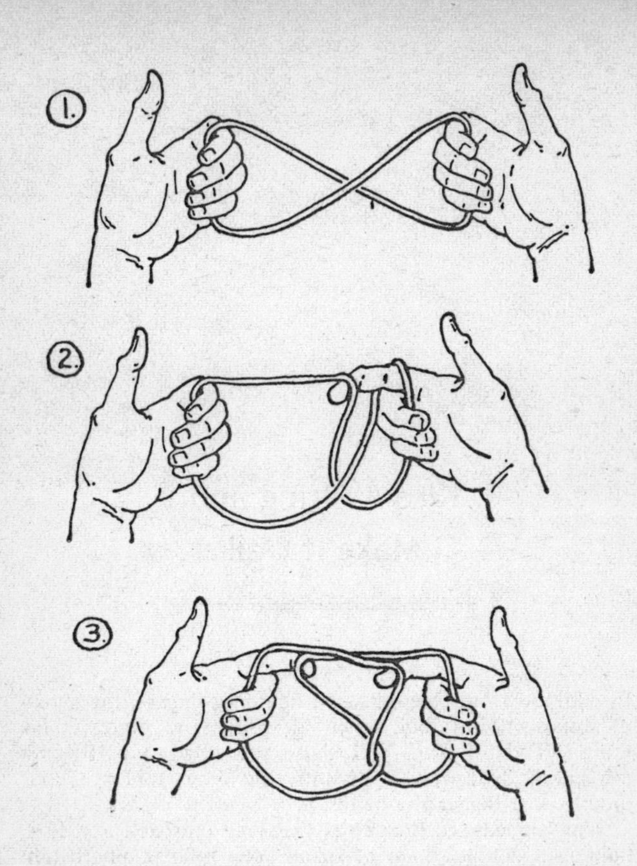

with your right hand and hold it in front of you as in figure 1.

Reach out with your right index finger and pick up the loop off your left hand (figure 2). Without dropping anything, now, reach out with your left index finger and pick up the loop off your right hand (figure 3).

See the sort of triangle opening up between your index fingers in figure 3? Reach in there with the remaining fingers of both hands and pull the doubled loop out. You now have figure 4, a double loop with the two loops joined as shown in the detail of figure 4.

Now then, the spot where the doubled loops are joined

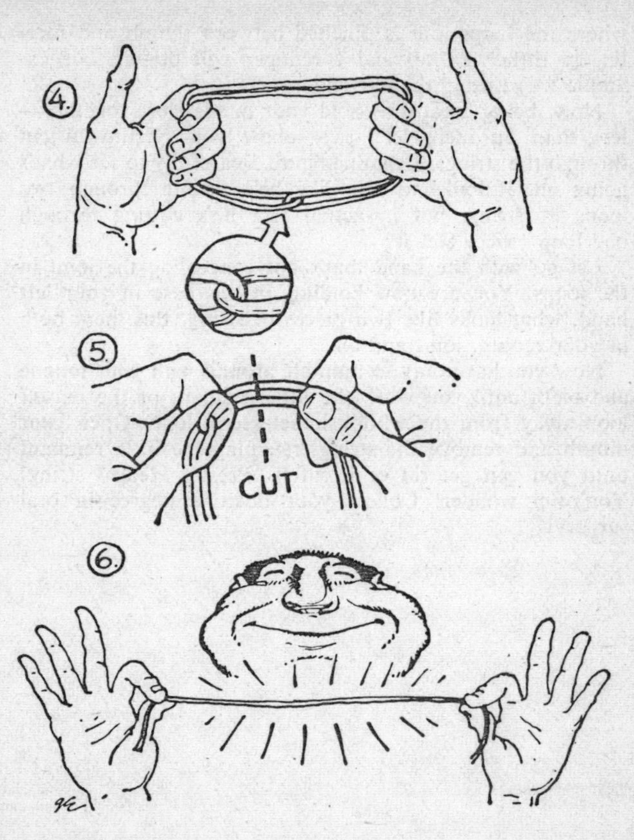

is the heart of the trick, and of course you don't want your victim to see it. Keeping it a secret is easier than it looks. Just practice doing steps 1 through 4 until you can do the whole thing in a single flowing motion, too quickly to follow. After all, you just say you're making a double loop of string and then you make it. Just before figure 4 is attained, you can "adjust" the loops by running the joined spot in the string toward one hand or the other. It's easy to get it out of sight behind one hand before you pull the two loops snug. All right, practice for a while and then we'll go on.

Ready? Keep on "adjusting" the loops until the spot

where the loops join is pinched between thumb and forefinger. Either thumb and forefinger will do—in our example we're using the left (figure 5).

Now, being careful to hold your hands close together—less than an inch, let's say—allow your victim to cut through the strings. Examine figure 5 carefully to see what's going on. It looks to him like he's cutting through two loops of string, but in actual fact he's cutting through one loop twice. Get it?

Let go with the hand that's not concealing the joint in the loops. You are now holding, in this case in your left hand, what looks like two pieces of string. Put them both in your mouth, joint and all.

Now you have only to mumble around with your tongue and teeth until you work the little remnant of the cut-off loop away from the wholly intact secret loop. Open your mouth and remove the string, retaining the little remnant until you can get rid of it safely. Presto! Healed string! You're a wonder! Collect your doctor's degree in oral surgery!

The Underhand Overhand Knot

All show-offs know how to tie an overhand knot in a piece of rope without ever letting go of the ends. Do you? If you think you do, get a piece of rope a couple of feet long, or a piece of string, or a rolled-up scarf or even a diaper, and try it for a while. Convinced?

All right, take a break. Stand around and lean on the wall a minute, and fold your arms as you relax. You know how people fold their arms when they're just standing around, right? You'd better, because that's the key to success. Just in case you have some doubts, simply put your left hand on your right biceps and then tuck your right hand between your left elbow and your chest. Your arms are now folded.

Now, get somebody to hand you the ends of your piece of rope, while your arms remain folded. Take one end in your left hand, which is easy; take the other end in your right hand, but be sure you don't move your hand to take it. You must grab the rope with your right hand under, not above, your left arm.

All right, you now have your arms folded and the ends of the rope in your hands. It remains only to unfold your arms without letting go of the rope. You can cry "Alakazam!" if you wish, but whether you do or not, a perfect overhand knot will appear in the rope as you unfold your arms.

If you have no friend to hand you the rope, it's possible to manage by putting the rope on a table and then bending over, arms folded, and picking up the ends by yourself. As soon as the neighborhood knows what you're up to, friends will come running.

Strung Up by the Buttonhole

There are a thousand mystifying tricks in the show-off's ball of string, and one of the best is this string maneuver we learned from Joseph C. Poley of Alden, Pennsylvania. All you need in order to do this trick is a shirt with at least one buttonhole in it and a loop of string about two feet long; please remember that the drawings here are only a sketch, and do not represent our opinion of what Mr. Poley really looks like.

Start in the position shown in figure 1, with the string loop stuck through your buttonhole and over both thumbs. Your mission, now, is to get the string out of the buttonhole without ever letting go of it. Try it for a while before you read the instructions. See the point?

All right, now proceed carefully or you may get tangled up and have to have your shirt slit off you. Be sure the loop of string is not twisted (see figure 1). Now, with your left pinkie, reach over to your right side and pick up the string behind your right thumb on your left pinkie (figure 2).

Do exactly the same thing with your right pinkie, reaching over to just behind your left thumb and picking

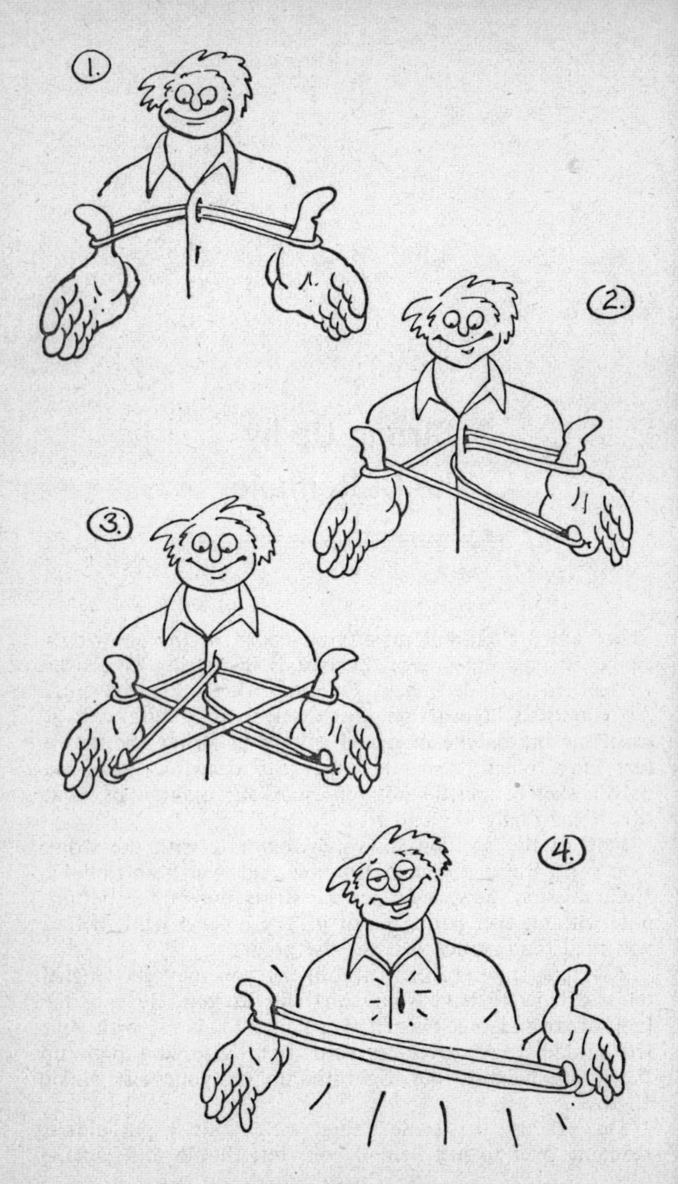
1.
2.
3.
4.

HOME DELIVERY AT HALF THE COVER PRICE!

Use This Label To Order **Newsweek**

(Mr. Mrs. Ms.) ______

Address ______ (APT.)

City ______ State ______

Zip ______ Please Initial Here ______

Enter my Introductory Subscription for 25 weeks at just $12.50

54205724

☐ I prefer 48 weeks at $24.00.

☐ Payment Enclosed ☐ Bill Me

(Put form in envelope)

Good Only in the 50 States of the U.S.A.

FIRST CLASS
PERMIT NO. 250
LIVINGSTON, N. J.

BUSINESS REPLY MAIL

NO POSTAGE STAMP NECESSARY IF MAILED IN THE UNITED STATES

POSTAGE WILL BE PAID BY

Newsweek
THE NEWSWEEK BUILDING
LIVINGSTON, N. J. 07039

up the string (figure 3). By this point you should feel pretty helpless, but rescue is in your own hands; you have only to let go of the string with your right pinkie and your left thumb. Now separate your hands (figure 4) and the whole thing slips from your buttonhole like a garter snake heading for the high grass, ZIP!

A word of complicated warning here; the illustrations are meant to show you how this trick will look to an observer, not how it will look in the mirror. However, like so many things in life, if you do it exactly backward it will work every bit as well. Also like so many things in life, you get much faster and better at it after a little practice.

The Four-Finger Escape

There are lots of handy tools for the show-off to establish his superiority with, but none more handy than the everyday common piece of string. Others may be rich, wise, powerful, ostentatious—but as long as the show-off has even a piece of string, he can do something others can't. Even a couple of shoelaces might work, in a pinch.

In the Four-Finger Escape, the performer, or exhibitionist, takes a loop of ordinary string and wraps the fingers of one hand up in it. He winds the string around his thumb, and then wraps up his fingers some more. Then, with a dazzling flash and a superior smile, he pulls on the string and it comes free. To all appearances, the string has metaphysically passed through the fingers. Or did the fingers pass through the string? How? Well, it's all in the wrapping. Follow the instructions very very carefully, or you'll truss your hand up like a cat in a knitting basket.

Start the Four-Finger Escape by tying about a two-foot piece of string in a loop. Hang it over your left little finger as shown in figure 1.

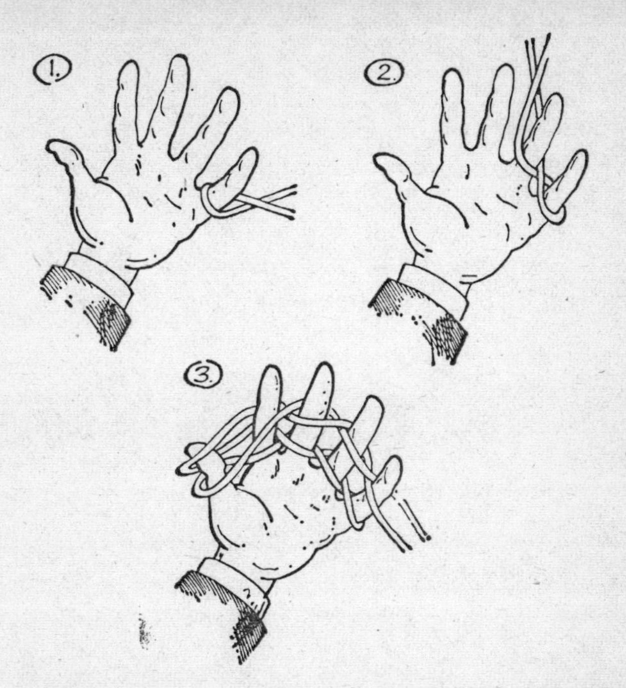

Now, starting from your little finger, wrap the loop around each finger in turn, as shown in figure 2. The loop gets a half-turn to the right every time it goes around another finger. Continue until you reach the forefinger; then, without any further twisting, bring both strings around the thumb from back to front, as shown in figure 3.

Cross the forefinger again and go back toward the pinkie, this time giving the loop a half-turn to the left at each finger. When you are finished, your hand should look exactly like figure 3. Study your hand and then study figure 3. Got it? If not, go back and start over.

When your hand agrees with figure 3, you're ready to escape. Just slip your thumb out of the loops by wiggling it a little. Then, pull with your right hand on the end of the string, and, with a mysterious motion, the string will slip right through the remaining fingers and you're free.

PART FOUR:

The Power To Cloud Men's Minds

Abusing the Imagination

One way the show-off can triumph is by exploiting the outer reaches of man's brain, that small corner of his head where his imagination lies. The stunts we're about to show require lots of imagination but very few props: a cloth napkin, a paper bag, a thread that does not exist, and a rubber ball that doesn't exist either (using props that don't exist is a great way to whip inflation).

Take, for example, the cloth napkin. In figure 1, the show-off holding the napkin has just said to the chump behind him, "Watch this. I will take this napkin and, with my fingernails, pick loose a thread from the weave and pull it out tight with my left hand." The man makes a few "attempts" to free such a thread (though he's actually engaging in clever misdirection, one of the show-off's great allies). He eventually "finds" a thread and pulls it loose. The chump can't really see it but assumes it's too thin to perceive with the naked eye—and that, friends, is what makes him a chump.

The show-off holds the napkin in his other hand, as shown in figure 2, cleverly concealing his thumb in the folded corner of the napkin. He coordinates the hand

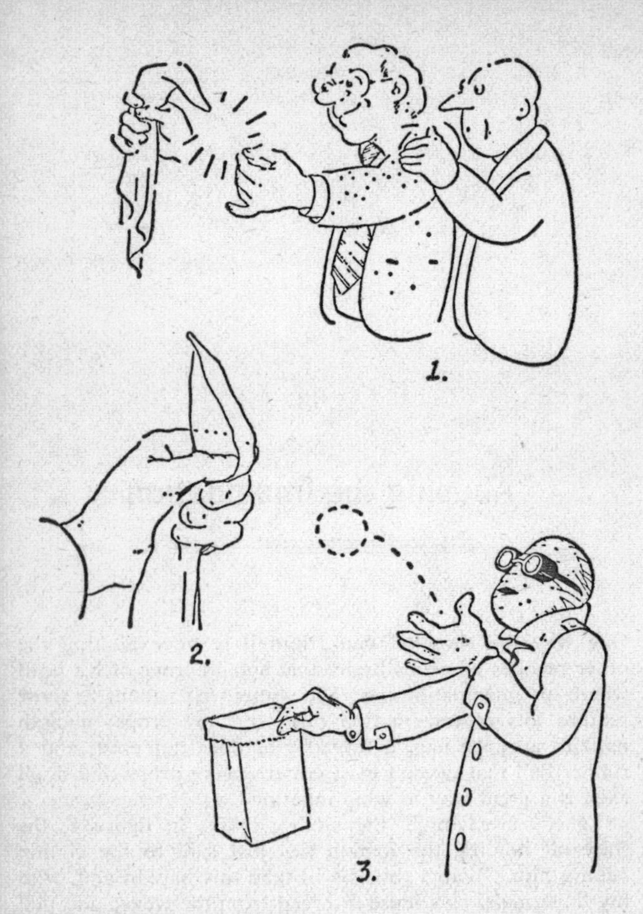

holding the "thread" with the wiggles of the thumb holding the napkin. When he pulls the "thread" the napkin moves with it. The effect is this: the chump gapes as the show-off manipulates the napkin to and fro. It's a wonderful ice-breaker at lunch or dinner.

A suggestion for advanced show-offs: After you have found the imaginary thread, try sticking it in one ear, then pulling it out the other. This way when you pull the thread you will be pulling it back and forth through your head—and the napkin will wiggle-waggle just as easily.

In figure 3 you see a man about to catch an imaginary ball in a brown paper bag. Whaat?! Here's the pitch: bounce a nonexistent ball several times. Then, as you hold a paper bag between your thumb and fingers—make sure you turn down a lip on the bag as shown—prepare to flip the ball up into the air. As the ball "descends," move the bag under it. When the ball reaches the bag, snap your fingers hard, making the bag go Pop!—just as it would if a real ball had actually fallen into it. The resulting illusion is wondrously convincing.

Off to Phone the Wizard

James Weaver, an art teacher in North Versailles, Pennsylvania, has this friend, see, a Wizard he calls from time to time. The Wizard has special powers of the mind—he can tell over the phone what card somebody holds in his hand miles away. Mr. Weaver puts a call in to the Wizard whenever he's in the mood to show off. He has most graciously decided to tell us—and you—the Wizard's phone number. Well, not really. Not actually the phone number but the low-down, inside poop on the Wizard. Here's how it goes.

Have a chump pick a playing card, any card, from a deck. Tell him you know this Wizard across town, a master of extra-sensory perception. The Wizard is so amazing he can identify the card over the phone. You dial the Wizard's number and say, "Hello. Is this the Wizard?" (Pause.) "May I speak to him then, please?" (Pause.) "Here he is"—and you hand the phone to your chump. The Wizard, speaking in a wizard-like voice, tells the chump what card he's holding. The Wizard then hangs up. Your chump drops his drawers.

Advanced show-offs may have already figured out that there ain't no Wizard, at least no Wizard with powers of

the mind. What there is is this—your accomplice, a friend who can be counted on to play the Wizard whenever you have a chump on the line. This is how it works:

As soon as the Wizard hears you say, "Hello, is this the Wizard?" he begins to recite the suits: hearts, diamonds, etc. As soon as he identifies the suit of the card your chump is holding, you break in and say, "May I speak to him then, please?" Now the Wizard starts running down the card numbers: deuce, three, four, five, etc. When he gets to the correct card, you cut him off, turn to your friend, saying, "Here he is . . ." Your chump says hello. The Wizard tells him the correct card and hangs up.

Maybe you're wondering: What friend is so loyal as to play the Wizard any hour of the day, any time it moves you to show off? You'd better be prepared to be his Wizard once in a while, even in the dead of night. It's the least you can do to gain glory.

How to Drive a Neat Person Crazy

The nice thing about showing off is that you can show off for everyone or show off for those certain types of people you think deserve a lesson or two. This trick will show you how to drive a very specific kind of person nuts, the thread-picker. You know the thread-picker—it's the person, man or woman (though usually a woman), who can't stand to see a piece of thread or lint or fuzz on your clothing. Nobody, of course, wants to have thread or lint on his clothing, but sometimes it's nonetheless annoying to have it picked off. This little ploy we're about to show you is the perfect comeback. It's an ancient ploy as timeless as the thread-picker himself (or herself).

The object in the box here is a flat sewing-machine bobbin, wound with whatever color thread you like. What you do with it is this: put the bobbin in the breast pocket of your jacket. Then, take the end of the thread and run it out of your pocket and through your lapel. Leave about an inch or so hanging out of the lapel. Then go to work or to school or to a party—or anywhere else you know you'll see friends, enemies and thread-pickers.

Sooner or later, somebody will be talking to you and

they'll spy the thread on your jacket. When they do, just keep talking and stay cool. After a moment or so, the thread-picker will do her thing: she'll reach out, take the thread, and try to pick it off your jacket. She'll pull on it and more thread will appear. Then more. If she's compulsive enough, she'll pull at least a foot of thread before getting the idea.

She'll think twice the next time she tries to clean up your act.

How to Be Telepathic

Every so often the show-off leaves the real world of torn phone books and crushed beer cans and enters the mysterious world of psychic phenomena. And that, folks, is where we're going right now. Fasten your seat belts for this amazing voyage through the brain, find an accomplice as well as a chump, plus nine ordinary playing cards, including two nines of any suit.

Inform your victim that he is to pick any of these nine cards and tell you which it is, and that you will "transmit" the identity of the card to the third person, your accomplice. You have, of course, previously arranged a deceptively simple ploy. Take a look at the drawing here. See the man touching a diamond on the nine of diamonds? That's you, and that's your ploy.

Your accomplice leaves the room. You lay out your nine cards in the H-pattern shown here. You ask your victim to pick a card—he picks, for example, the seven of spades. Your accomplice returns. You inform the accomplice that a card has been picked, and that you will concentrate hard on that card in order to send a psychic message. Then, starting anywhere you like, you go around the H-pattern, touching each card and asking your accomplice, "Is this it? Is this it? Is this it?" And so on.

The key lies in the nines. For when you touch the first nine you come to, touch it on the figure that corresponds to the card in the H-pattern; as you can readily see, the spades or diamonds or hearts or clubs on a nine are arranged in the same H-pattern as your larger layout on the table. By touching the correct diamond you signal the placement of the chump's selected card—in this case, the seven of spades. You use two nines so that your accomplice can't fail to pick up your clue.

When the accomplice proclaims, "Yes, that's the one. That's his card!" your victim will be dumbfounded. He'll ask that you do it again. You do. You will feel the rush of supreme glory once again.

High, Wide Handies

There are many low forms of wit—puns, moron jokes, etc.—but the lowest and most annoying, without doubt, is the Handy. About every ten years a wave of Handies, those mysterious gestures that the show-off performs, and then invites the onlooker to guess what they are, sweeps the country. It's been several years since the last invasion, so the show-off is well advised to prepare himself now. Be the first on your block to have a ready repertoire of Handies, so that when conversation lags you'll have something left to say with the two paws nature gave you!

Figure 1 shows how the Handy works. At a critical moment in midoperation, the famous surgeon drops his tools, joins his right forefinger and thumb together, wiggles the other fingers furiously, and sweeps the whole gesture in a wide arc from his left to his right. Just when the bystanders notice there's something wrong, the famous surgeon demands: "What's this?"

Naturally, nobody knows what this is. With a shout of triumph, the famous surgeon exclaims: "I don't know either, but here it comes again," and repeats the gesture. All the bystanders faint—some with admiration, others with outrage. To the show-off motivation doesn't matter, as long as they react!

Now, try figure 2. Place the palm of one hand on the

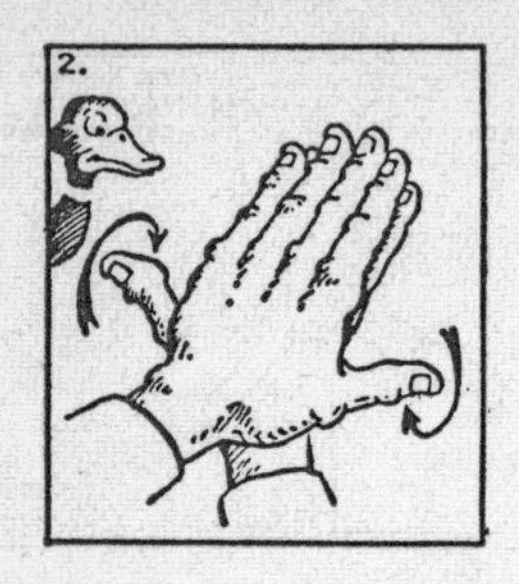

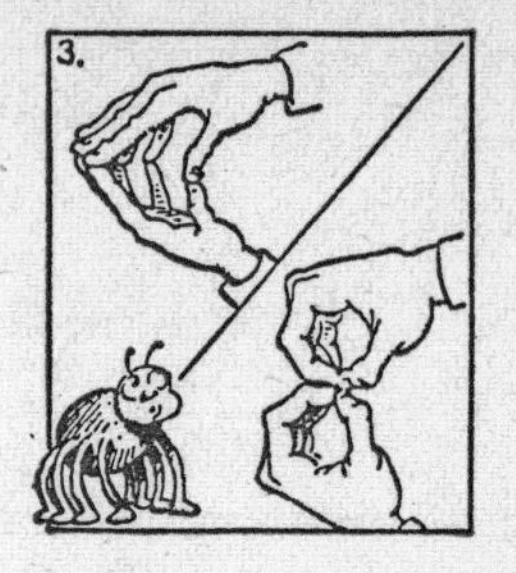

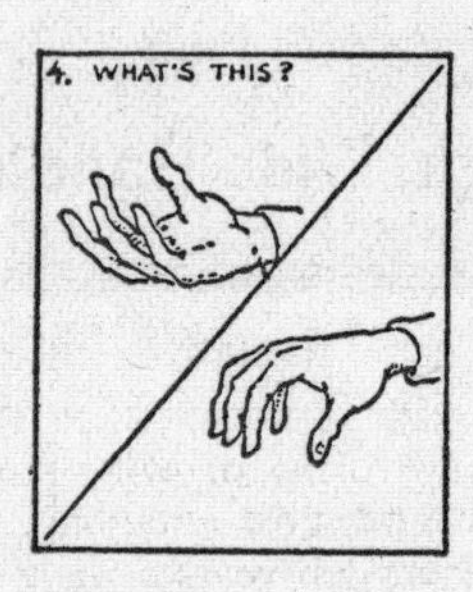

back of the other, rotate the thumbs madly, and sweep the whole affair forward gracefully through the air. Shout out: "What's this?" "We don't know," the world will reply. "A duck with an automatic transmission!" you exclaim. Groan!

Figure 3 shows both stages of the Handy you explain to an anguished audience as "A spider doing push-ups on a mirror."

Figure 4, the greatest of the classical Handies of the past, works like so: "What's this?" you demand, showing your palm up with the fingers slightly curled.

"I don't know," your victim confesses as he grits his teeth.

"THIS, DEAD!" you snap as you exhibit the same gesture right-side-up, so to speak.

From here the show-off proceeds to create Handies of his own. For example, use a gesture of your own invention and ask what it is. When they give up, declare it's "elephant repellent."

"There are no elephants around here," they're sure to object.

"You see, it works!" you cry, and start running.

How to Be an Easy Ace at Tennis

Let us begin by admitting the best way to show off is to be actually good at something. The surest way to glory and success is skill. But since not many of us really have skill, it might pay to start looking around for what's second best. What's second best is style. For even if you do things lousy, you can always score a few points with your style.

Perhaps, for example, you sometimes play a little tennis. If so, chances are you are an average weekend tennis player. This means that for every set you win, your opponent wins a set. And for every easy slam you sock into the net, your opponent will sooner or later match you.

Such play is fun, no doubt, and certainly good exercise. But don't you sometimes get impatient? Don't you sometimes want to look better than your skill allows? Some players try to look better by buying expensive tennis outfits and shiny steel rackets. Our suggestion is more subtle. Try showing off by knowing how to pick up errant balls without bending over. This gives the impression you are being casual about the whole affair—and makes losing a lot less embarrassing. Below are two easy ways of being graceful on the court, a lot more graceful than any of your shots.

Side-of-the-foot method: The duffer you see here is about to pick up a ball with his foot. He has just fanned on an easy lob and checked out his racket for holes. Now he will recoup. He walks over to the ball and, using his racket, rolls it up to his foot. He keeps the racket against the ball and, in one graceful lift, brings the ball up between racket and foot. With a deft kick, the ball is popped into the air, and the player catches it nonchalantly with his free hand. The ball is now in the hand used to toss it up for serving. That's it. One easy motion, no bending, no sweat. The player might now strike a yawn to enhance the effect.

Shovel method: Another way to pick up a ball is to shovel it with your racket. The three drawings here show the important steps. Place your racket over the ball, as in the top drawing. Pull your racket toward you with a quick jerk of the wrist, as in the middle drawing. This action

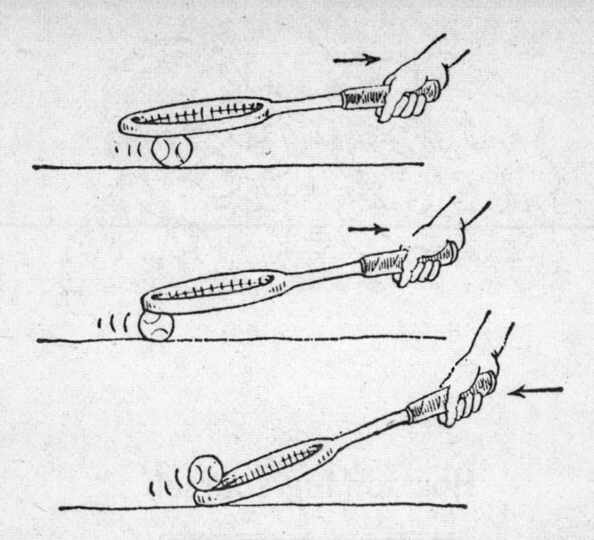

permits you to then get your racket under the ball with a quick forward motion of the wrist (see bottom drawing). Now all you need to do is flip the ball into the air and catch it with your free hand.

How to Mug Yourself

An infallible way to get other people's attention is to commit violence on them. Nobody can ignore you if you kick them in the shins. The trouble with showing off by hitting people is that if they're big and powerful they hit you back; and of course it's exactly the big and powerful whose attention the show-off most desires.

A much safer way to make everybody look at you is to commit violence on yourself. You probably already know how to crack your knuckles, for instance, and you know how impossible it is for anyone to ignore knuckle-cracking. Well, the same goes in spades for the art of nose-cracking. Get a grip on your proboscis and hang on while we tell you how to do it.

Here's the effect: after announcing that you're about to break your nose, stand and face your audience. Look them in the eye, and place one hand on either side of your nose, as in figure 1. You bend your nose a little to the right, then a little to the left, just to loosen it up, you say. You give it maybe a couple more flexes to get it nice and soft. Then you twitch it firmly to one side or the other—always leaving your hands in place—and it emits a loud, sharp CRAACK! You'll never know till you try it how sick this will make everybody watching. They'll beg you never to do it again! Of course, you do it again, right away.

So how do you do it? See figure 2. The actual noise of flesh and bone splintering is made simply by dragging your thumbnails across the edge of your front teeth with a sharp snap. Of course, in real life the position of your hands conceals your thumbnails so people think it's really your nose breaking off. The longer your thumbnails, the louder the noise.

On your way out of the room you can make everybody feel a lot better if a mysterious hand grabs you by the throat and gives you the punishment you deserve. The mysterious hand, of course, is yours, cleverly arranged, as the picture of the man in the doorway shows.

The Mystic Magnetic Sex Detector

See the bald-headed mad scientist in the picture? Like all show-offs, he's using his secret powers to baffle and astonish other people by pulling stunts they can't understand. In this case, he's demonstrating how the sex of a human being can be determined by using the Mystic Magnetic Sex Detector—which is nothing more than a ring (or any other small weight) attached to a couple of feet of ordinary string.

Of course, the Mystic Magnetic Sex Detector isn't really mystic, and it isn't magnetic either. What it is, is an age-old demonstration of the fact that beliefs can influence actions, even unconsciously.

Here's how it works: you suspend the ring over the palm of a human being of either sex. Then you set the ring to swinging in a gentle arc. If the palm belongs to a female, the swings of the ring will, after a few seconds, settle into a circular pattern (figure A). If, on the other hand, the subject is male, the ring will soon begin to swing back and forth, more or less in a straight line (figure B). That is—and this is very important—the ring will do this if you believe it will!

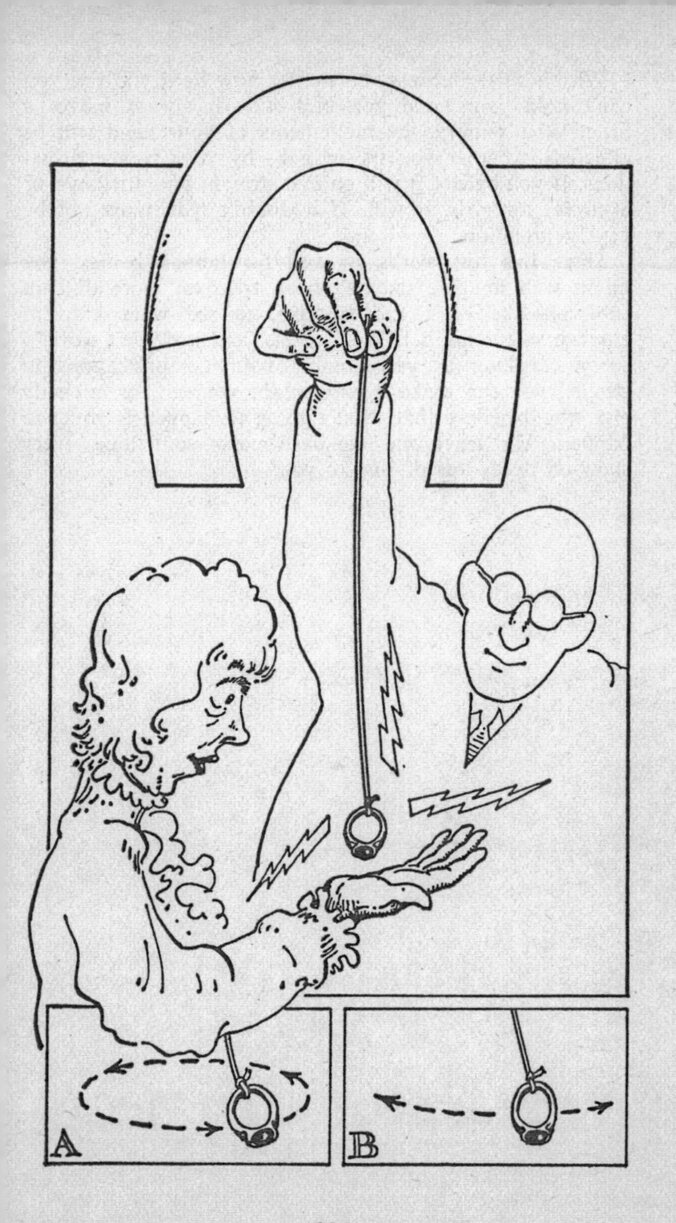
A
B

Why is this? Because, no matter how hard you try, you can't hold your hand perfectly still—it always moves a little. What's more, the movements of your hand will be affected—whether you try or not—by your own expectations. If you believe it will go in a straight line, for boys, or a circle, for girls, it will. If it doesn't, you must not be paying attention.

Since this test works so well for human beings, you might well imagine that it's been tried on more difficult subjects—like eggs, for example, to see what kind of chicken will come out. Well, it has, and it doesn't work—sorry. So long as you confine your demonstrations to people, you can make it happen for yourself, or anybody else who'll believe that what's going to happen is going to happen. We leave the persuasiveness—something every show-off needs lots of—up to you.

The India Rubber Pencil

A show-off's whole career is based on creating one big illusion—making people think you're smarter, more graceful, and more accomplished than you actually are. Such an illusion, if persisted in, becomes true in the long run, especially if you begin to believe it yourself. But like all big illusions, it's made up of a lot of little illusions. Watch this one carefully, please.

Nothing can make you feel more powerful than making people see things that aren't really there—pink elephants, for example, or flying saucers. Pink elephants and flying saucers are hard to conjure up; but India rubber pencils are all over the place, waiting for you to create them. To make one, start with the ordinary pencil of your choice, the longer the better; no stubs, please. Better yet, borrow a pencil from the nearest available victim, hold it up in front of his face, and tell him you're going to turn it to rubber. This he won't believe, take it from us—at least not until, with a few deft wiggles of your accomplished hand, he sees the pencil flex up and down like crazy—or like rubber.

How is it done? It's all in how you wiggle the pencil. Hold it loosely by one end, between forefinger and thumb,

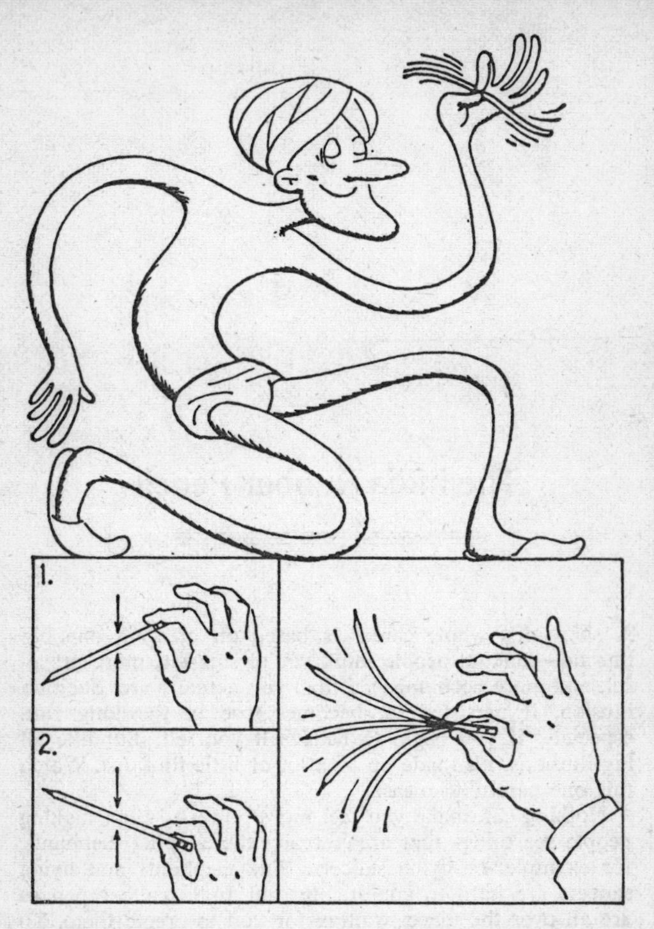

as shown in figures 1 and 2. Note the arrow pointing to the center of the pencil. Now, as you wiggle the pencil up and down, holding it loosely, your hand rises and falls in the identical but opposite rhythm. Figure 1 shows the top of the stroke, figure 2 the bottom. Try it; you'll get the hang of it in about a second.

The third drawing shows, not what actually happens, but what a spectator sees—or thinks he sees. The whole effect is owing to persistence of vision, the same phenomenon that allows you to see, among other things that aren't really there, movies that seem actually to move.

Once you've learned to make rubber pencils, it's up to you to find uses for them, like signing checks that are going to bounce anyway. Just don't stick them in your ears.

PART FIVE:

Looky What You Made!

The Egg Rocket

One of the first show-offs recorded by history was the Greek physical philosopher Hero of Alexandria, who may have lived as early as the second century B.C. He invented the very first jet-propelled device, the aeolipile, which ran round and round like crazy, driven by jets of expelled steam, without ever getting anywhere. To make your own name famous forever, like Hero's, it is only necessary to construct this modern jet-propelled equivalent of his invention.

Take two eggs, and extract their contents either by (a) punching one tiny hole in one end of each egg and sucking out the egg, or (b) punching one tiny hole in both ends of each egg and blowing them empty. Method b is easier, but if you use it you must seal one hole with a small square of aluminum foil and some kind of glue that will resist heat and dampness (figure 1); Lepage's Liquid Solder is good for this purpose (although not perfect; follow instructions on the tube and hope for the best).

Take a large cork and drive a large pin or needle right through the middle (figure 2). Stick a couple of small forks firmly into opposite sides of the cork and then, carefully,

using soft copper wire from the hardware store, suspend the eggs from the ends of the forks and a pair of metal thimbles below the eggs. Your final product will not be as neat as this drawing may lead you to think is possible; don't worry. Just wrap everything up in copper wire until it's secure.

The eggs should be firmly attached to the ends of the forks and the thimbles solidly suspended below the lowest points of the eggs. Be sure that the open holes in the ends of the eggs face in the same angular direction—i.e., either clockwise or counterclockwise. Now, lay this assembly aside for a moment.

Finish the main bearing for the machine by drilling a small hole about halfway through a penny, for the end of the needle to rest in. Now, either glue the penny directly on the mouth of a large, heavy bottle—too large and heavy to tip easily—or glue it to a cork that fits the bottle (figure 3).

Assemble the machine, now, by placing the egg-and-fork structure carefully on top of the bottle and bearing. Very likely it will tilt to one side, out of balance. Adjust the balance either by pulling out one of the forks and replacing it in the cork, or by wrapping more wire around the end of the lighter fork, or both, until the balance is achieved.

To load the rockets, it's necessary to get some water inside the eggs. This is hard! Use a fine-pointed eye-dropper, a model railroader's oiler, or a model builder's glue gun to get maybe a half teaspoon of water inside each egg. When you're convinced there's some in there, stoke the thimbles by stuffing them lightly with cotton, then soaking the cotton with denatured alcohol. You may be tempted to use lighter fluid, but don't; it smokes some-thing awful.

Take the whole contraption to a safe place, like a big tile bathroom or a concrete basement floor, far, far from anything that might catch fire. Assemble the machine and recheck the balance, adjusting as necessary. Finally, light both thimbles with a match.

After a few minutes, the water in the eggs will begin to boil, and steam will rush from the holes in the eggs, caus-ing the whole thing to spin madly with a great hiss. Ours attained about forty revolutions per minute at top speed; yours may do better. Warning: if you let the eggs run dry inside, the glue patching the sealed pair of holes will fail and you'll have to start all over again.

Once you're convinced it works, call in any jet pilots who live in the neighborhood and astonish them by doing anything they can do, with the help of two eggs and the will to show off.

A Hanky Is a Hanky Is a Rose

If you're respectable enough to carry a handkerchief, you can be even more respectable after we tell you how to take an ordinary pocket handkerchief (a clean one, please) and form it into a rose of unspeakable beauty. Remember this the next time someone of the opposite sex asks for your hanky. Instead of giving her a plain handkerchief, give her a veritable flower.

Take your square handkerchief and, as in figure 1, fold over a corner to the middle. Repeat this folding for each of the corners and you will wind up with a newly-formed square.

Do exactly the same thing once again, a folding process that will yield the form shown in figure 2.

And repeat still another time. Figure 3 shows the same folded hanky, this time one step smaller.

Now take your folded handkerchief and turn it over. Fold the corners the same way as before, as shown in figure 4.

Pick up the hanky by the pointy part (figure 5) and turn it over, with the palm of your hand facing up.

Now gently pull out the "petals," making a blossoming, fluffy flower. Your final rose should look as wonderful as the one in the drawing (figure 6).

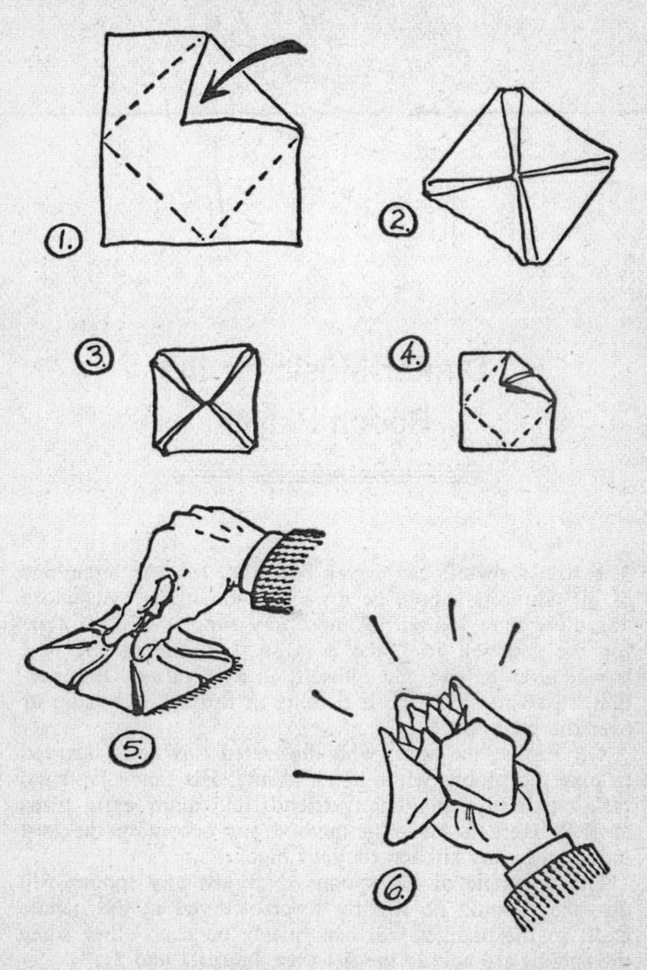

Dinner Music for the Spoon Player

The true show-off can never be quiet, lest the attentions of his admirers should be drawn to something even more attractive than himself. Almost any time is a good time for the show-off to make a noise, but one of the best is whenever he can add himself, as a private rhythm section, to whatever music is coming in through the radio or over the juke box.

Gil Eisner, the artist who illustrated this book, learned to play the spoons while in the Army. His fancy jug-band rat-a-tats earned him many friends and many extra turns at K.P. Here is his easy method for becoming the best musician in any kitchen on your block.

Get a couple of big spoons. Not just any spoons will do—they should be slightly reverse-curved at the handle ends, so the handles will bear nicely on each other when the spoons are held in the fist (see figures 1 and 2).

Spoons shaped for eating are not necessarily the best ones for sweet music. In figure 1, the top spoon is shaped the way it comes from the spoon factory. For performance

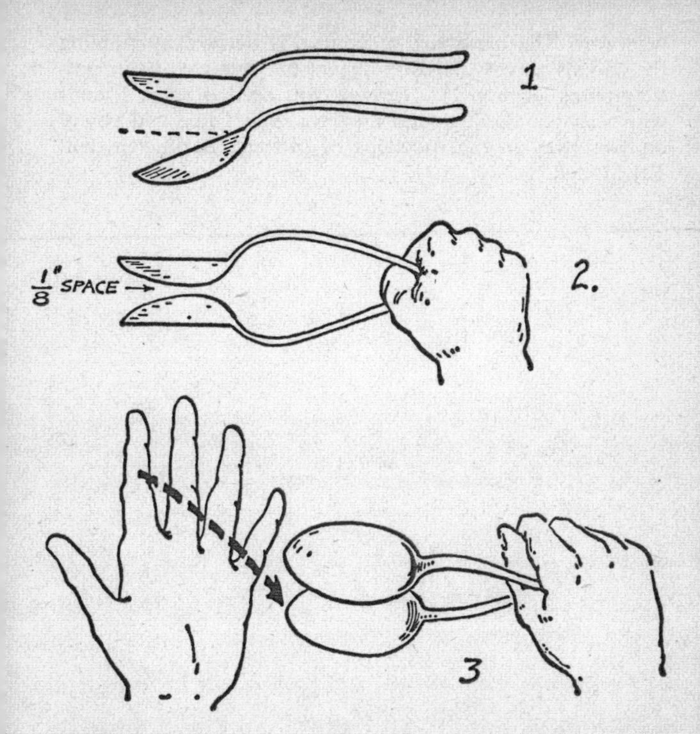

purposes, bend the bowl of the spoon down, maybe fifteen degrees, as shown in the bottom half of figure 1. Treat the other spoon likewise. It is best not to do this with your mother's good silverware. Use something cheap from the dime store.

Grasp the spoons gently but firmly in your fist as shown in figure 2, with one handle passing above your thumb and one below. The handles of the spoons should be in contact inside your fist, the bowls of the spoons about an eighth of an inch apart.

All right, now softly bop something with one of the spoons. Notice how the bowls come together with a sharp plunk, then spring apart ready for another plunk? There is your basic spoon rhythm stroke. Now turn on the radio and listen for something to join in with. All kinds of elegant variations are possible, as you pass the dancing spoons over the backs of your knees, the top of your hand, and wherever. The basic riff, of course, is derived by rippling the spoons across the four fingers of your free hand, rattlety-plunk (figure 3). Now all you need is some friends with washboards, jugs and maybe a bass fiddle and you're on your way in the footsteps of Mozart, Beethoven, and Taj Mahal.

The Betsy Ross Five-Pointed Caper

Now that our nation has had its Bicentennial, show-offs rejoice to remember that the United States is the greatest show-off country on earth. The legend of showing off in America records this topping stunt by Betsy Ross, maker of our first flag: when George Washington went to call on Betsy Ross to ask her to make a flag, he presented her with a sketch of what he had in mind.

"All the stars have six points," said Betsy.

"So what?" said George.

"Five points is prettier," she replied.

"Yes," said George, "but six points is easier to make."

"Not for me!" cried Betsy, and showed off then and there by snatching a piece of white cloth, folding it a couple of times, and snipping once with her scissors to produce a perfect five-pointed star. And that's why we have the flag we have today, instead of one less pretty. Now here's how Betsy did it. Get a piece of paper (or cloth) and a pair of scissors and be like her.

Take a piece of paper—8½ by 11 typing paper is fine—and hold it vertically as in figure 1. Fold once in half (figure 2). Now, take what you have after performing figure 2, and make a mark at the midpoint of the left-hand side (the easiest way to do this is by folding in half once more, as in figure 3, and creasing lightly just at the left edge, then flatten it out again back to the configuration of figure 2).

Fold the lower right-hand corner to the midpoint of the left edge (figure 4) and crease. Now, see figure 5; take the right-hand edge of what you made in figure 4 and fold it down and to the left until it too crosses the midpoint on the left along the new edge created in figure 4. Crease.

Now, fold the left bottom corner upward and crease as in figure 6.

With the scissors, cut along the imaginary dotted line

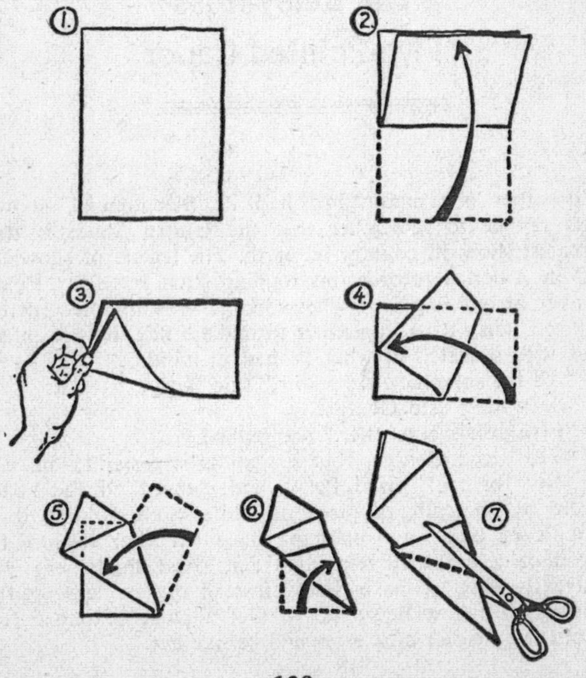

shown in figure 7. Unfold the paper and there you have it. Repeat fifty times and you have enough stars for the whole country, including Alaska and Hawaii. If there are any states you don't like, you can leave them out.

Curse of the Cootie-Catcher

The purpose of the cootie-catcher—a folded-paper gadget formerly found in every American third-grader's school desk but now falling into disuse—is to stupefy your friends by showing them that their hair is full of little black bugs, or cooties. What you do after that depends on how fast you can run, or how good your friends really are. A reasonably adept show-off should be able to handle the consequences gracefully. Now, here's how to handle the preliminaries, by making a cootie-catcher.

Take a full-size sheet of typing paper and fold one corner over to the opposite edge to make a square (step 1). Cut or tear off the remainder, keeping the square part (step 2).

Lay the square flat and fold each corner to the exact center of the square, creasing each fold (step 3). Turn the result over, and fold each corner to the center of the square again (step 4). Crease the folds firmly.

You now have step 5, and from here on out is where you have to be careful. You need two more sharp creases, vertical and horizontal, which you get simply by folding step 5 in half—first from top to bottom, then from side to

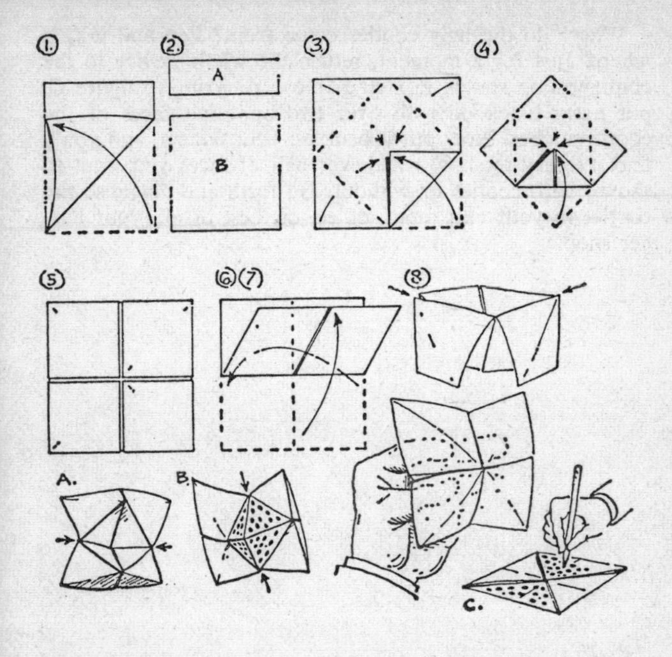

side (steps 6 and 7). In each case, make a sharp crease, then return to step 5.

Now, take the step 5 object, suitably creased, and push, do not fold, two opposite corners toward each other, as the two arrows show in step 8. The whole thing should snap into a sort of crown-shaped affair, with triangular corners, into the back of which you can insert your thumb and fingers as the shadow-line drawing below step 8 shows. One finger to each corner, except that your fourth and pinky fingers go together.

You are now almost, but not quite, ready to catch cooties. Study the method of operation of the completed cootie-catcher, as shown in figures A and B. Notice that the cootie-catcher is hinged in two planes at right angles to each other (see the arrows in A and B?). You approach a victim holding it open, as in A. You clap it swiftly to his head and exhibit the result, as in B. Ugly black dots all over! Argh, you cry, an infestation of horrible cooties. Off to the showers with your friend.

Where do the ugly cooties come from? Pen and ink, is where. Just for a moment, return the whole device to the configuration shown in step 5. Now, referring to figure C, put nasty black dots all over two opposing faces of the cootie-catcher. Now put it back on your fingers, and you'll find it's easy to show whichever pair of faces you want to show—with cooties or without. Go forth and diagnose the cooties in your classroom, office, or, best of all, your barber shop.

Up and Down with the Cartesian Devil

The nasty little creature in the picture, with the long tail and the diving mask, is not really the hero of this chapter. The real Cartesian Devil is the gadget at his right—a gadget which has its place in demonstrating some laws of physics, but whose actual purpose is to enable you to baffle your friends with your cleverness by exerting your mysterious powers to make the floating eyedropper in the bottle rise, sink, or hover in the middle at your word of command. Of course, you have to cheat to make it happen, but you probably expected that.

To make a Cartesian Devil, get three things: (1) a clear, flexible plastic bottle of the kind that shampoo or dish detergent comes in; soak the label off; (2) a plastic eyedropper; (3) an inch or so of soft wire—plain copper is good, but soft solder is better, because it's softer.

Fill up the bottle with water. Wrap the wire around the end of the dropper so it will float in a stable position, end down. Now, put enough water in the eyedropper so that, when dropped in the bottle, it just barely, and we mean barely, floats. The rubber end of the dropper should

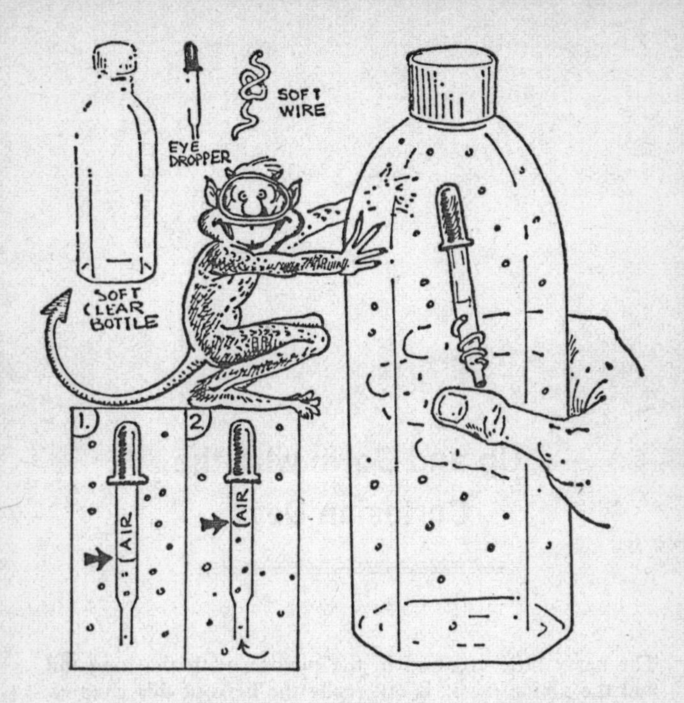

scarcely break the surface. Adjust the amount of water in the dropper until you have it right.

Screw the top on the bottle. You are ready. Pick up the bottle and give it a squeeze. Amazing! The eyedropper sinks to the bottom. Stop squeezing and the dropper rises.

When showing off in public, of course, you'll want to hold the bottle at arm's length, while making mysterious gestures with your free hand to convince the ignorant that your psychic powers are doing the trick for you.

What's really doing the trick for you? Glad you asked. Since air can be compressed and water can't, when you squeeze the bottle something has to give. And the only air in the bottle is contained in the top of the eyedropper. So the floating dropper (detail 2) becomes the sinking dropper when you squeeze the bottle, compressing the air in the dropper and causing more water to enter through the hole in the bottom (detail 2). The soft rubber bulb on the dropper has nothing to do with the case, it's only a convenient means of adjusting the amount of water in the dropper. So that's the theory. As for why the thing is called a Cartesian Devil, we don't know. If you're any kind of real show-off, you should be able to make up a story about it without any more help from us.

The Moebius Strip Tease

Germany is not a land notable for show-offs. Slow and steady is more the German style (though they don't mind making show-off equipment, like Porsche cars, for Americans). Nevertheless, the lightning from heaven that makes a show-off can strike anywhere, and one day in 1858 it descended on the mathematician August Ferdinand Moebius, who was sitting around his library in Leipzig cutting out paper dolls and such-like. Suddenly, Moebius rose like a shot from his armchair and cried: "Donnerwetter! I have invented a piece of paper like the world has never seen before. Fame and glory are mine!"

Moebius was right; he is now known worldwide for inventing the Moebius Strip, a piece of paper with truly astonishing properties. You can astonish your immediate vicinity by doing what Moebius did; simply take a strip of paper about two feet long (the long way of an unfolded sheet of newspaper is about right), give it one-half turn as shown at the top of the illustration, and tape or paste A to B, so as to produce a loop of paper with half a twist in it.

What is so remarkable about this loop? Well, for one thing, it has only one side and only one edge, as you can

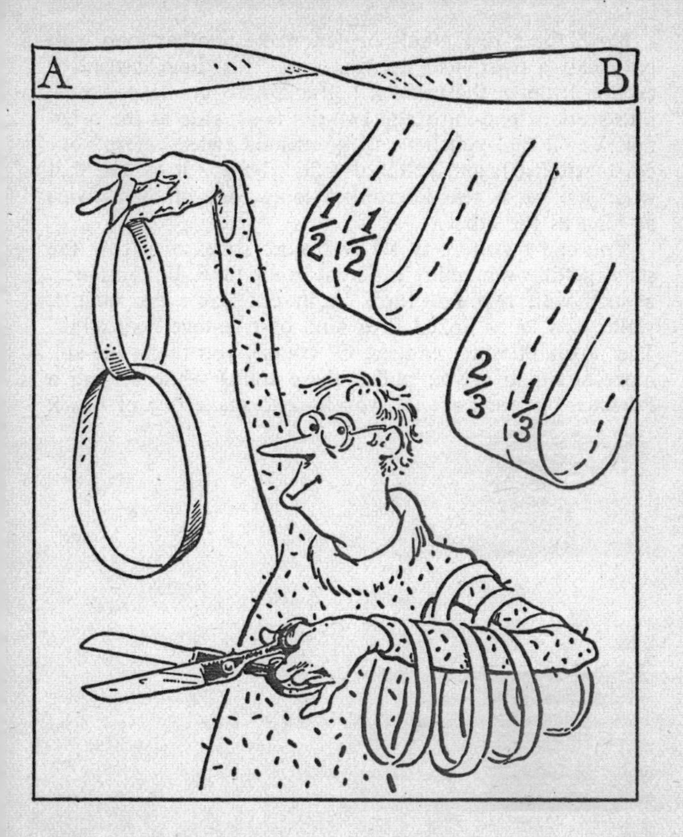

easily prove by drawing a line down the middle until it meets itself. More remarkable is what happens when you take a pair of scissors and cut down the line, dividing the paper half-and-half. Go ahead. You were expecting maybe that by cutting one loop in two you would get two loops? No such thing! You get one loop twice as long as the one you started with!

More surprises are possible. Instead of making a half-twisted loop, give the paper one full turn before sticking the ends together. Then cut down the middle. Result: two loops all right, but interlinked. If you have a sharp enough eye, you can split each of the two loops for a total of four interlinked loops.

Now, for a real mind-boggler, make another loop with only half a twist, like the first one. This time, instead of cutting it down the middle, half-and-half, cut to one side, into sections one-third and two-thirds as wide as the original. You'll find you have to go around twice before your cut meets itself; and you'll also find, believe it or not, that what you get is two interlinked loops, one of them twice as long as the other.

You can try more twists and more styles of slicing the strip, getting something different every time. For instance, a strip with two full turns in it, cut down the middle, yields two loops linked in a kind of true-love-knot affair. The possibilities are endless. Of course, you might get still more attention if you pulled these stunts while driving a Porsche, but we can't tell you how to make one of those.

The Coffee-Can Boomerang

Even show-offs would live in a better world if there weren't so much junk lying around, right? People who litter the earth with old tin cans are not show-offs, just slobs.

When the show-off throws away a tin can, it doesn't just lie there. No sir! It comes right back! Then the show-off lovingly picks it up, dusts it off, and puts it on the shelf with the rest of his show-off equipment. Here's how to build the mysterious returning tin can and fascinate everybody on your block, especially the hound dogs.

Collect an ordinary coffee can (empty), two big matches (or sticks about the same size), an office rubber band, and a couple of lead wall anchor plugs from the hardware store (or big fishing sinkers, or anything that's small and heavy). Punch a hole right in the middle of each end of the coffee can—the fixed end, and the lid. See figure 1 for the correct arrangement.

If you're using lead anchor plugs, fasten them together with a hefty piece of tape (figure 2) and then tape them to the middle of the rubber band (figure 3). If you have a big sinker, just put it in the middle of the rubber band with a knot.

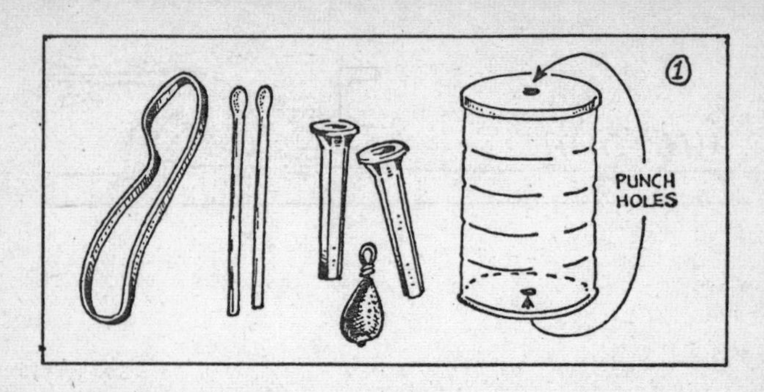

Thread the rubber band through the holes in the ends of the can, and hold it there with the match sticks (figure 4). The rubber band should be tight enough to keep the weights from striking the sides of the can, when the can is in a horizontal position.

When everything is finished as in figure 4, just roll the can away from you. This will take a stronger and smoother push than you think. Now watch! As the can rolls away, the weights wind up the rubber band. The can stops. Then it rolls right back to you. Fantastic.

For a superior, more mysterious version of the coffee-can boomerang, you could conceal the presence of the rubber band by screwing two screw-eyes in two small blocks of wood, gluing the blocks to the inside of the can-lids with epoxy, and stringing the band between the hooks. But maybe you'd better not. If you show off too brilliantly, even the dogs will begin to resent you.

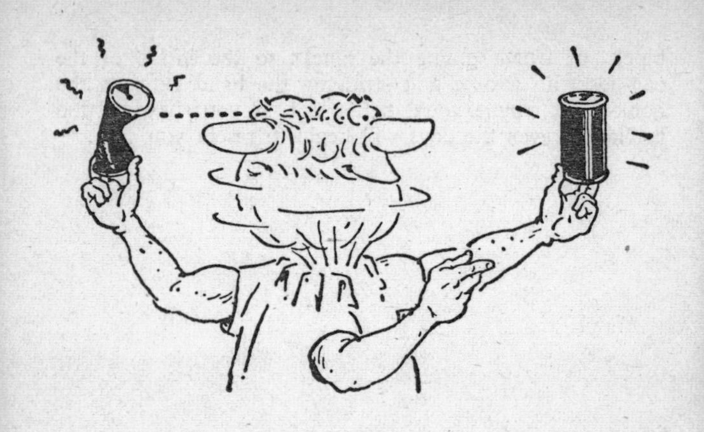

How to Uncrush a Beer Can

Much have we travelled in the realms of gold, fellow show-offs, and we've revealed to you many a mystery, but by all the odds the most useful was when we showed you how to crush a steel beer can in that wonderful, indispensable book *Sneaky Feats* (published by POCKET BOOKS in 1976). Now, assuming you know how to crush a beer can, we're going to show you, for a change, something perfectly useless and, in its slow-moving way, equally spectacular: how to *uncrush* a beer can. For this purpose, we've adopted the method used by Francis Galton, author of the nineteenth-century classic *The Art of Travel,* for taking the dents out of canteens. Canteens are few and far between, these days, and they don't dent because they are made of plastic. But a classic is a classic, and this knowledge must not perish from the earth.

First, crush a beer can. This time, don't use one of the hard-to-find but totally superior steel kind; get the ordinary, new-fangled aluminum sort, because it works better.

And don't crush it too much; enough will be enough. Just make your point; batter it up good but don't destroy it.

Take your crushed beer can and fill it up, through the hole, right to the brim with dried split peas—yellow or green, makes no difference. When it won't hold any more, pour some water in until it won't hold any more water either. Put it in the sink, right side up. After about an hour, add some more water to replace any that's soaked into the peas.

Nothing will happen for what seems an eternity. Then, after two or three hours, the peas begin to swell up. With irresistible force, the peas will expand. With little shrieks and creaks, the knocks and dents in the beer can will be ironed out by the expanding peas.

Finally, the swelling peas will restore the can to its original pristine condition. If this doesn't quite happen, shake and scrape out the peas and give it a refill and some more time.

Once you start the peas swelling, it is unnecessary, of course, to touch the can with the human hand again. This is the point at which to place your bets; the strongest person you know will be unable to do with both hands what you can do with none, if only you've got some peas and some patience.

The Explorer's Needle

Suppose you're misplaced in Africa or some other confusing part of the earth, don't speak the local language, and wish to know which way is north. If that's too much supposing, just suppose you're messing around the house on a rainy day and want to exhibit your mastery of the principles of surface tension and magnetism to an admiring audience of one or more. Whichever you'd rather suppose, here's a snazzy way to suppose it, with the help of a few simple household articles.

For the first part of this stunt we thank Dave Black of Fort Wayne, Indiana, who points out that if you are very careful you can make a needle (or a straight pin) float in the surface tension on top of a glass of water. Since many straight pins are made of nonmagnetic brass, use a steel needle if you want to proceed to part two.

For part one, all you do is fill up a glass of water, let it settle quietly, and gently, gently, place a small steel needle flat on top of the water. Miraculous! It floats! If your hand isn't steady enough to make it float, do what Dave

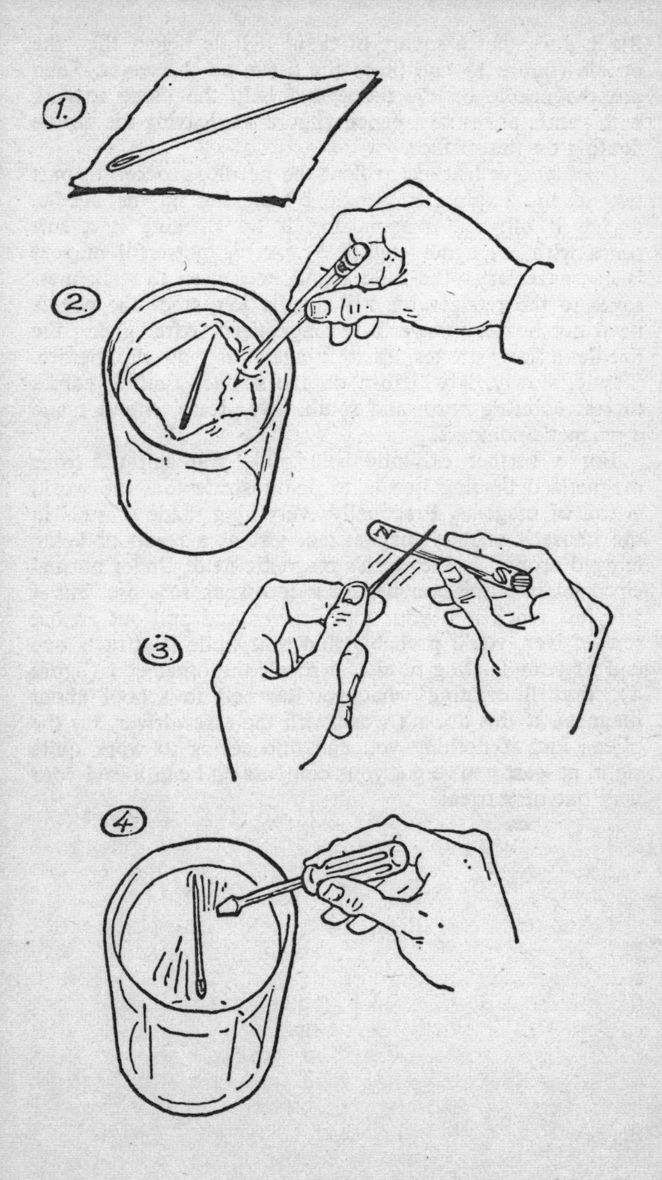
1.
2.
3.
N
S
4.

Black does: cut a square of tissue a little bigger than the needle (figure 1) and place the tissue on the water. Then put the needle on the tissue and help the tissue to sink with gentle pokes of a pencil (figure 2), leaving the needle floating on the surface.

Once you've learned to float the needle, proceed to part two of the Explorer's Needle by picking up the needle, drying it off, and magnetizing it by stroking it a few times with a magnet (figure 3). A big powerful magnet is not necessary—the little round ones used to stick messages to the refrigerator will do the job, since the needle need not be very powerfully magnetized. After giving the needle a few strokes, float it again as you did before. Slowly, slowly, it will turn on the surface until it comes to rest pointing north and south, and presto, you've made a magnetic compass.

For a further exhibitionistic trick, you can use your magnetized floating needle to demonstrate that the world is full of magnets. Practically everything made of steel in the house is slightly magnetized, just as a result of being banged around in the earth's magnetic field. Under normal circumstances this magnetism is too weak to sense, but if you just reach into your tool drawer and pull out an old screwdriver, you'll probably find that while it attracts one end of your floating needle, it repels the other end (figure 4), thus illustrating what you learned in school about magnets. If this doesn't work with the screwdriver, try the pliers; and if nothing you can find seems to work quite right, at least you've got your compass and can locate your way out of Africa!

The Kwick-'n'-Eezy Filet de Boeuf Wellington

Everybody envies a great cook, one of those people who can, at vast expense and with infinite skill and labor and careful attention to Escoffier, whip up a great classic specialty like Beef Wellington—that tender filet bathed in delicate mushrooms and the very best goose-liver pâté, all wrapped up in flaky pastry and done to tender perfection. To be a great cook takes a lifetime of hard work—too hard for show-offs. Everybody will envy you almost as much if you can just fake it in about half an hour with easy everyday ingredients. Here's how to be envied almost as much as a great cook, and produce results nothing short of spectacular. So what if the Galloping Gourmet can do better?

Buy the tail end of a filet of beef—about a one-pound chunk. Cut the fat (figure 1) out of the middle, and soak the meat for a while in Lea & Perrins sauce, or a superior marinade of your own devising, if you insist. Tie it up with string, rolling into a shapely chunk (figure 2). Note that this is not rolled end-to-end like a jelly roll, just sideways until snug.

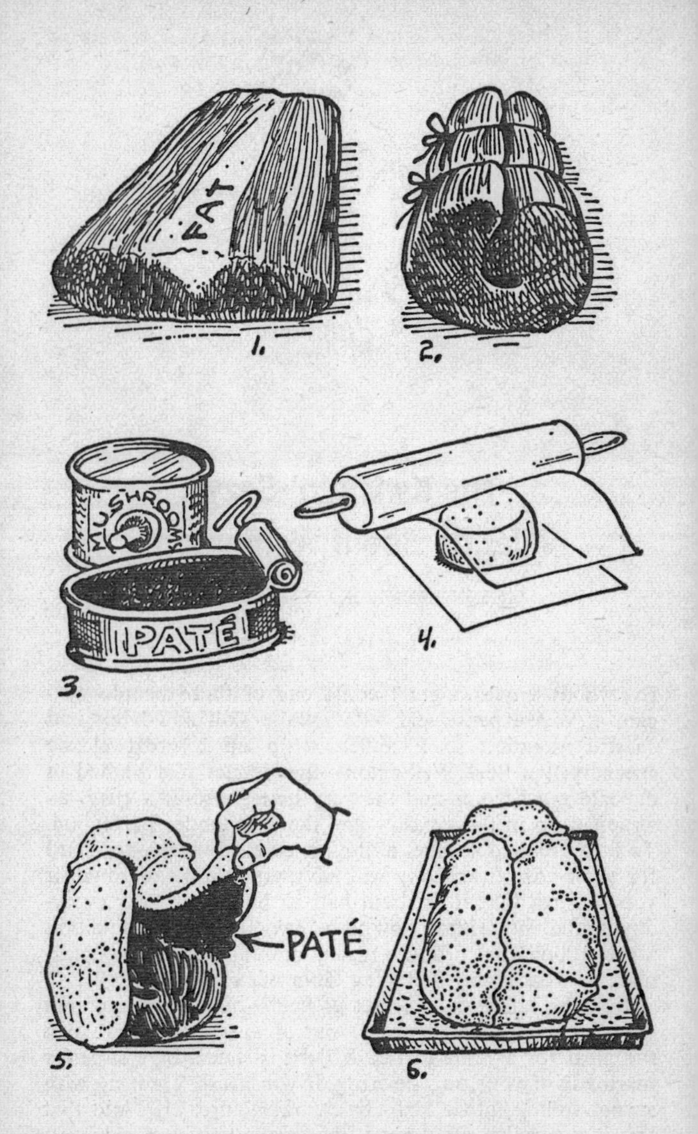
FAT
1.
2.
MUSHROOMS
PATÉ
3.
4.
PATÉ
5.
6.

Put the beef in a pan and stick it in a very hot oven for about four minutes, to set the shape of the meat. Meanwhile, take a four-ounce can of mushrooms (or fresh if you can get them), drain and blot dry with a towel, chop very fine, and mix them up with a four-ounce can of liver pâté—the quality is up to you (figure 3).

Quick, now, open a can of refrigerator biscuits, put a biscuit between two sheets of waxed paper and roll it flat, into a long oval (figure 4), about as long as the meat. Spread the biscuit with some of the pâté-mushroom goo, untie the meat, and put it on the pâté-spread biscuit. Roll out more biscuits and wrap them around the meat, like tiles, first spreading the meat with the pâté mixture (figure 5).

Notice how the meat has a sort of V-shaped slot on top? Fill the V with the mushroom goo, and keep tiling the meat with rolled biscuits. As you go, seal the edges of the biscuits by squeezing them gently together. It helps if you don't get the edges slippery with pâté mixture. Milk can be used for glue to help hold the edges together.

When the whole filet is tiled up, cook at 450 degrees on a big flat pan until the outside is well browned. The meat will be rare and tender, and the whole thing will resemble one of those lumpy knotted breads you see in German bakeries (figure 6).

To serve, slice with a very sharp knife and just, well, serve. Go ahead and let everybody at dinner think it's just bread, until, with a flourish of your razor-keen carver, you reveal your tantalizing surprise and emit the show-off's war cry: "I bet you can't do this!"

Acknowledgments

We would like to recognize the contributions of our friends, correspondents and relations toward making this book what it is today. Our thanks pour forth to the following exhibitionists, many of whom deserve better things than being put on a list like this. We hope they get them:

Dave Black (The Explorer's Needle)
Jeff Brown (Kiss a String and Make It Well)
Carmen Buccola (Look, Ma, One Hand)
Gil Eisner (Dinner Music for the Spoon Player)
Sarah Ferrell (How to Mug Yourself)
Ken Geisel (The Invaluable One-Dollar Ring)
Joseph C. Poley (Strung Up by the Buttonhole)
Bruno Profumo (Slipping the Cuffs)
James Weaver (Off to Phone the Wizard)
Otho C. Woods (The Five-Cent Solution)